THE SOCIAL TEACHING OF POPE JOHN XXIII

THE SOCIAL TEACHING
of
POPE JOHN XXIII

REV. JOHN F. CRONIN, S.S., Ph.D.
ASSISTANT DIRECTOR, DEPARTMENT OF SOCIAL ACTION
NATIONAL CATHOLIC WELFARE CONFERENCE

THE BRUCE PUBLISHING COMPANY
MILWAUKEE

NIHIL OBSTAT:

Harry A. Echle
Censor

IMPRIMATUR:

✠ Patrick A. O'Boyle
Archbishop of Washington
August 5, 1963

Library of Congress Catalog Card Number: 63–22039

To the Memory of Pope John XXIII
Father and Teacher to All Mankind

PREFACE

THE brief but glorious span of the pontificate of Pope John XXIII bequeathed to the world many rich legacies. Notable among these are two social encyclicals, the masterful and progressive *Mater et Magistra* (Christianity and Social Progress) and the historic *Pacem in Terris* (Peace on Earth). This book extracts from these documents, in topical fashion, excerpts of passages that advance Catholic social thought in the socioeconomic field. Excluded from this selection are points covered by preceding pontiffs and a few items that have minor relevance to social and economic life.

Excerpts are grouped in the same order as that used in the author's 1959 work, *Social Principles and Economic Life*. Indeed, the selections and comments are the equivalent of a major revision of this earlier work. Thus, in Chapter XV, "Racial Discrimination and Racial Justice," there are only a few encyclical excerpts, but an extended commentary on revolutionary developments in race relations. By contrast, when the selections cover matters treated in the earlier book, they are treated quite briefly and the reader is referred to the previous study. In short, the present work presupposes the development of Catholic socioeconomic thought provided in *Social Principles and Economic Life* as a background for appreciating the fresh direction given by Pope John.

Accordingly, the two books must be considered as complementary. It is planned to merge them when the time is ripe for a major revision of *Social Principles and Economic Life*. Such a revision would be premature at this writing, largely because there has been considerable pressure to include pronouncements on social issues in the decrees of Vatican Council II. Should these be forthcoming, they would become a part of the revised text.

Readers are advised to study the full text of both encyclicals, but especially to ponder "Peace on Earth." This is probably the clearest, most orderly, and best translated of all social encyclicals. The N.C.W.C. translation, used in the text, is recommended as the most accurate in terms of the official Latin. For "Christianity and Social Progress" the preferred translation used here is by Rev. H. E. Winstone, as adapted by *The Pope Speaks*. This excels in literary style and is reasonably accurate. Those seeking a more literal version may prefer the Paulist Press — N.C.W.C. edition, translated by Rev. William Gibbons, S.J.

REV. JOHN F. CRONIN, S.S.

CONTENTS

THE SOCIAL TEACHING OF POPE JOHN XXIII

Chapter I

THE SOCIAL QUESTION

SOCIAL CONDITIONS IN 1891

Mater et Magistra

10. Leo XIII spoke in a time of social and economic upheaval, of heightening tensions and actual revolt. Against this dark background, the brilliance of his teaching stands out in clear relief.

11. As is well known, the outlook that prevailed on economic matters was for the most part a purely naturalistic one, which denied any correlation between economics and morality. Personal gain was considered the only valid motive for economic activity. In business the main operative principle was that of free and unrestricted competition. Interest on capital, prices — whether of goods or of services — profits and wages, were to be determined by the purely mechanical application of the laws of the market place. Every precaution was to be taken to prevent the civil authority from intervening in any way in economic matters. The status of trade unions varied in different countries. They were either forbidden, tolerated, or recognized as having private legal personality only.

12. In an economic world of this character, it was the might of the strongest which not only arrogated to itself the force of law, but also dominated the ordinary business relationships between individuals, and thereby undermined the whole economic structure.

13. Enormous riches accumulated in the hands of a few, while large numbers of workingmen found themselves in conditions of ever increasing hardship. Wages were insufficient even to the point of reaching starvation level, and working conditions were often of such a nature as to be injurious alike to health, morality, and religious faith. Especially inhuman were the working conditions to which women and children were sometimes subjected. There was also the constant specter of unemployment and the progressive disruption of family life.

14. The natural consequence of all this was a spirit of indignation and open protest on the part of the workingman, and a widespread tendency to subscribe to extremist theories far worse in their effects than the evils they purported to remedy.

SOCIAL CONDITIONS TODAY

Mater et Magistra

46. In the twenty years which have elapsed since the changing economic climate noted at that time by Pius XII the economic scene has undergone a radical transformation, both in the internal structure of the various states and in their relations with one another.

47. In the field of science, technology, and economics we have the discovery of nuclear energy, and its application first to the purposes of war and later, increasingly, to peaceful ends; the practically limitless possibilities of chemistry in the production of synthetic materials; the growth of automation in industry and public services; the modernization of agriculture; the easing of communications, especially by radio and television; faster transportation and the initial conquest of interplanetary space.

The social and political fields

48. In the social field we have the development of social insurance and, in the more economically advanced communities, the introduction of social security systems. Men in labor unions are showing a more responsible awareness of major social and economic problems. There is a progressive improvement in basic education, a wider distribution of essential commodities, greater opportunities for advancement in industry and the consequent breaking down of class barriers, and a keener interest in world affairs shown by people of average education.

At the same time, however, this assessment of the increased efficiency of social and economic systems in a growing number of communities serves also to bring to light certain glaring discrepancies. There is, in the first place, a progressive lack of balance between agriculture on the one hand, and industry and public services on the other. Secondly, there are areas of varying economic prosperity within the same political communities. Finally — to take a world view — one observes a marked disparity in the economic wealth possessed by different countries.

49. To turn to the political field, We observe many changes. In a number of countries all classes of citizens are taking a part in public life, and public authorities are injecting themselves more each day into social and economic matters. We are witnessing the break-away from colonialism and the attainment of political independence by the peoples of Asia and Africa. Drawn together by their common needs nations are becoming daily more interdependent. There is, moreover, an ever extending network of societies and organizations which set their sights beyond the aims and interests of individual countries and concentrate on the economic, social, cultural, and political welfare of all nations throughout the world.

Millions in dire straits

68. We are filled with an overwhelming sadness when We contemplate the sorry spectacle of millions of workers in many lands and entire continents condemned through the inadequacy of their wages to live with their families in utterly subhuman conditions. This is probably due to the fact that the process of industrialization in these countries is only in its initial stages, or is still not sufficiently developed.

69. Nevertheless, in some of these lands the enormous wealth, the unbridled luxury, of the privileged few stands in violent, offensive contrast to the utter poverty of the vast majority. In some parts of the world men are being subjected to inhuman privations so that the output of the national economy can be increased at a rate of acceleration beyond what would be possible if regard were had to social justice and equity. And in other countries a notable percentage of income is absorbed in building up an ill-conceived national prestige, and vast sums are spent on armaments.

70. In economically developed countries, relatively unimportant services, and services of doubtful value, frequently carry a disproportionately high rate of remuneration, while the diligent and profitable work of whole classes of honest, hard-working men gets scant reward. Their rate of pay is quite inadequate to meet the basic needs of life. It in no way corresponds to the contribution they make to the good of the community, to the profits of the company for which they work, and to the general national economy.

260. This era in which we live is in the grip of deadly errors; it is torn by deep disorders. But it is also an era which offers to those who work with the Church immense possibilities in the field of the apostolate. And therein lies our hope.

Pacem in Terris

156. In fact, all human beings ought rather to reckon that what has been accomplished is but little in comparison with what remains to be done: because organs of production, trade unions, associations, professional organizations, insurance systems, legal systems, political regimes, institutions for cultural, health, recreational, or athletic purposes — these must all be adjusted to the era of the atom and of the conquest of space, an era which the human family has already entered, wherein it has commenced its new advance toward limitless horizons.

POPE JOHN issued his first social encyclical for the purpose of bringing Catholic social teaching up to date. Much had happened since his predecessors pronounced on these problems in 1891, 1931, and 1941. Men of science released nuclear energy, developed synthetics, made automation possible, and began the conquest of space. There were important social and political changes as well. Advances were scored in social security and public education. The older forms of colonialism were dead. Men participated more widely in the affairs of nations and even in international matters. Progress was evident on all sides. One could dream that science and technology would abolish want.

But this progress is highly uneven in its impact. Millions in Asia, Africa, and Latin America live in poverty, even in destitution. Even in the wealthier and more industrialized nations, there are pockets of great need. Some regions remain underdeveloped. Certain classes of citizens fail to share in the general wealth of prosperous countries. Often there is stark contrast between the luxury of the few and the privations of the many.

It is a matter of particular concern that frequently workers are not yet paid wages according to the social contribution made by their toil. The entertainment field often pays fabulous salaries. In return, sports heroes furnish passing diversion to their followers. Motion-picture stars may pander to sensuality and debase popular ideals of family life. Even scientific research is becoming almost a military monopoly, demanding billions in contrast to the few millions devoted to medical research.

No wonder, then, that the present age can be characterized in terms of extreme possibilities. It is "in the grip of deadly errors; it is torn by deep disorders. But it is also an era which offers to those who work with the Church immense possibilities in the field of the apostolate. And therein lies our hope."

Hope is the theme running through both these encyclicals. Pope John was the very essence of Christian optimism. He preferred to stress the positive, not the negative. He was not blind to the evils of the world, but he chose to use the limited time of his pontificate to encourage harmony and progress, rather than indulge in denunciation. He promoted love, joy, and trust, while he abjured fear, hatred, and suspicion. These traits of character made him loved by the whole world, but they were more than personal characteristics. They sprang from deep intellectual conviction and hence pervaded his social teaching. Pope John was more than a man of extraordinary virtue, he was also a teacher possessing consummate skill. These qualities become increasingly evident, as we probe into his detailed prescriptions for the modern world.

For earlier papal references and commentary, see Social Problems and Economic Life, Chap. I, pp. 3–9, 16–19.

Chapter II

THE CHURCH AND THE SOCIAL PROBLEM

Mater et Magistra

2. Christianity is the meeting point of earth and heaven. It lays claim to the whole man, body and soul, intellect and will, inducing him to raise his mind above the changing conditions of this earthly existence and reach upward for the eternal life of heaven, where one day he will find his unfailing happiness and peace.

3. Hence, though the Church's first care must be for souls, how she can sanctify them and make them share in the gifts of heaven, she concerns herself too with the exigencies of man's daily life, with his livelihood and education, and his general, temporal welfare and prosperity.

179. Now, in bringing people to Christ, the Church has invariably, both now and in the past, brought them many social and economic advantages. For true Christians cannot help feeling obliged to improve their own temporal institutions and environment. They do all they can to prevent these institutions from doing violence to human dignity. They encourage whatever is conducive to decency and virtue, and strive to eliminate every obstacle to the attainment of this aim.

180. Moreover, in becoming as it were the lifeblood of these people, the Church is not, nor does she consider herself to be, a foreign body in their midst. Her presence brings about the rebirth, the resurrection, of each individual in Christ; and the man who is reborn and rises again in Christ never feels himself constrained from without. He feels himself free in the very depth of his being, and freely raised up to God. And thus he affirms and develops that side of his nature which is noblest and best.

EARLIER popes have stated eloquently the reason why the Church is interested in social problems. They have also made the claim that virtuous living leads to economic progress. But *Mater et Magistra* tends to be more specific on these points. It shows how a Christian is to approach the world about him, to bring it under God's law.

Historians might question the unqualified claim that the Church brings social and economic advantages to people. In recent centuries, most Catholic nations were economically backward. Those who trace the origins of capitalism to the eleventh century argue that many of the first capitalists rebelled against religious control. Weber and Tawney found elements in Protestantism that led to the Commercial and Industrial Revolutions. Yet, in contemporary Europe, social Catholicism is among the factors favoring the economic rebirth of the Continent.

This paradox might be explained by noting that, in the period between the Reformation and *Rerum Novarum*, the Church tended to be defensive and restricted in its engagement with the world. Where Catholics remained isolated in their ghettos, they could hardly influence society. Pope John would have the Catholic Christian transform the world, and not be preoccupied with fleeing its temptations.

His suggestions are concrete and practical. We are to examine the effect of our environment on human dignity. We prevent or remedy conditions, such as slums or racial discrimination, that do violence to human dignity. We do not seek all at once to attain some distant ideal, but rather we encourage whatever is conducive to decency and virtue.

Above all, we permit ourselves to be fully reborn in Christ and thus to be free in the very depths of our being. When we have given ourselves wholly to God, the noblest and best in our nature will emerge. Spontaneously we will be generous, kind, and compassionate. We will have the courage that comes from disinterested love. Having these qualities, we will become a powerful influence for good.

Why was this not the case in recent centuries? Because we were under the bondage of fear, and did not feel the freedom of sons of God. As the Church progresses in her inner renewal, more and more of her sons will acquire this Pauline sense of freedom. They will then be true apostles of the world.

See Social Principles and Economic Life, Chap. II.

Chapter III

MAN AND ECONOMIC LIFE

THE NATURE OF MAN

Pacem in Terris

9. Any human society, if it is to be well ordered and productive, must lay down as a foundation this principle, namely, that every human being is a person, that is, his nature is endowed with intelligence and free will. Indeed, precisely because he is a person he has rights and obligations flowing directly and simultaneously from his very nature. And as these rights and obligations are universal and inviolable they cannot in any way be surrendered.

11. Beginning our discussion of the rights of man, we see that every man has the right to life, to bodily integrity, and to the means which are necessary and suitable for the proper development of life; these are primarily food, clothing, shelter, rest, medical care, and finally the necessary social services. Therefore a human being also has the right to security in cases of sickness, inability to work, widowhood, old age, unemployment, or in any other case in which he is deprived of the means of subsistence through no fault of his own.

13. The natural law also gives man the right to share in the benefits of culture, and therefore the right to a basic education and to technical and professional training in keeping with the stage of educational development in the country to which he belongs.

Every effort should be made to ensure that persons be enabled, on the basis of merit, to go on to higher studies, so that, as far as possible, they may occupy posts and take on responsibilities in human society in accordance with their natural gifts and the skills they have acquired.

30. In human society, to one man's right there corresponds a duty in all other persons: the duty, namely, of acknowledging and respecting the right in question. For every fundamental human right draws its indestructible moral force from the natural law, which in granting it imposes a corresponding obligation. Those, therefore, who claim their own rights, yet altogether forget or neglect to carry out their respective duties, are people who build with one hand and destroy with the other.

87. Very often, experience has taught us, individuals will be found to differ enormously, in knowledge, power, talent, and wealth. From this, however, no justification is ever found for those who surpass the rest to subject others to their control in any way. Rather they have a more serious obligation which binds each and everyone to lend mutual assistance to others in their efforts for improvement.

THE SOCIAL NATURE OF MAN

Mater et Magistra

219. Individual human beings are the foundation, the cause, and the end of every social institution. That is necessarily so, for men are by nature social beings. This fact must be recognized, as also the fact that they are raised in the plan of Providence to an order of reality which is above nature.

220. On this basic principle, which guarantees the sacred dignity of the individual, the Church constructs her social teaching.

Pacem in Terris

31. Since men are social by nature they are meant to live with others and to work for one another's welfare. A well-ordered human society requires that men recognize and observe their mutual rights and duties. It also demands that each contribute generously to the establishment of a civic order in which rights and duties are ever more sincerely and effectively acknowledged and fulfilled.

16. The family, grounded on marriage freely contracted, monogamous and indissoluble, is and must be considered the first and essential cell of human society. From this it follows that most careful provision must be made for the family both in economic and social matters as well as in those which are of a cultural and moral nature, all of which look to the strengthening of the family and helping it carry out its function.

SOCIALIZATION

Mater et Magistra

59. Certainly one of the principal characteristics which seem to be typical of our age is an increase in social relationships, in those mutual ties, that is, which grow daily more numerous and which have led to the introduction of many and varied forms of associations in the lives and activities of citizens, and to their acceptance within our legal framework. Scientific and technical progress, greater productive efficiency, and a higher standard of living are among the many present-day factors which would seem to have contributed to this trend.

60. This development in the social life of man is at once a symptom and a cause of the growing intervention of the state, even in matters which are of intimate concern to the individual, hence of great importance and not devoid of risk. We might cite as examples such matters as health and education, the choice of a career, and the care and rehabilitation of the physically and mentally handicapped.

It is also partly the result, partly the expression of a natural, well-nigh irresistible urge in man to combine with his fellows for the attainment of aims and objectives which are beyond the means or the capabilities of single individuals. In recent times this tendency has given rise to the formation everywhere of both national and international movements, associations and institutions with economic, cultural, social, sporting, recreational, professional, and political ends.

Advantages and disadvantages

61. Clearly, this sort of development in social relationships brings many advantages in its train. It makes it possible for the individual to exercise many of his personal rights, especially those which we call economic and social and which pertain to the necessities of life, health care, education on a more extensive and improved basis, a more thorough professional training, housing, work, and suitable leisure and recreation. Furthermore, the progressive perfection of modern methods of thought-diffusion — the press, cinema, radio, television — makes it possible for everyone to participate in human events the world over.

62. At the same time, however, this multiplication and daily extension of forms of association brings with it a multiplicity of restrictive laws and regulations in many departments of human life. As a consequence, it narrows the sphere of a person's freedom of action. The means often used, the methods followed, the atmosphere created, all conspire to make it difficult for a person to think independently of outside influences, to act on his own initiative, exercise his responsibility, and express and fulfill his own personality. What then? Must we conclude that these increased social relationships necessarily reduce men to the condition of being mere automatons? By no means.

Creation of free men

63. For actually this growth in the social life of man is not a product of natural forces working, as it were, by blind impulse. It is, as we saw, the creation of men who are free and autonomous by nature — though they must, of course, recognize and, in a sense, obey the laws of economic development and social progress, and cannot altogether escape from the pressure of environment.

64. The development of these social relationships, therefore, can and ought to be realized in a way best calculated to promote its inherent advantages and to preclude, or at least diminish, its attendant disadvantages.

65. To this end, a sane view of the common good must be present and operative in men invested with public authority. They must take account of all those social conditions which favor the full development of human personality. Moreover, We consider it altogether vital that the numerous intermediary bodies and corporate enterprises — which are, so to say, the main vehicle of this social growth — be really autonomous, and loyally collaborate in pursuit of their own specific interests and those of the common good. For these groups must themselves necessarily present the form and substance of a true community, and this will only be the case if they treat their individual members as human persons and encourage them to take an active part in the ordering of their lives.

66. As these mutual ties binding the men of our age one to the other grow and develop, governments will the more easily achieve a right order the more they succeed in striking a balance between the autonomous and active collaboration of individuals and groups, and the timely co-ordination and encouragement by the state of these private undertakings.

True purpose of the economy

73. In view of the rapid expan-

sion of national economies, particularly since the war, there is one very important social principle to which We would draw your attention. It is this: Economic progress must be accompanied by a corresponding social progress, so that all classes of citizens can participate in the increased productivity. The utmost vigilance and effort is needed to ensure that social inequalities, so far from increasing, are reduced to a minimum.

74. From this it follows that the economic prosperity of a nation is not so much its total assets in terms of wealth and property, as the equitable division and distribution of this wealth. This it is which guarantees the personal development of the members of society, which is the true goal of a nation's economy.

246. Certainly, the Church teaches — and has always taught — that scientific and technical progress and the resultant material well-being are good things and mark an important phase in human civilization. But the Church teaches, too, that goods of this kind must be valued according to their true nature: as instruments used by man for the better attainment of his end. They help to make him a better man, both in the natural and the supernatural order.

THERE is no need to comment at length on the listing of human rights excerpted from *Pacem in Terris*. We only note that the list quoted above is selective, concentrating on rights connected with the economic and social order. The full text (Nos. 9–38) should be read, since no previous papal document contains such a clear and exhaustive compilation of man's rights and duties in society.

SOCIALIZATION

When *Mater et Magistra* was released, its qualified advocacy of socialization caused a minor tempest. The term was used in the unofficial modern-language translations issued by the Vatican, but it was replaced by various circumlocutions in the official Latin text. Much of the controversy, however, was the result of hasty reporting and headline writing. Socialization, as used by the Vatican translators, simply reflects the fact that modern life is becoming more social. Men are increasingly interdependent. The trend toward growing governmental controls over business is but one phase of this development. Actually the appraisal of this trend by Pope John was not substantially different from those of his predecessors.

There was some difference, and this fact is important in assessing the function of papal social encyclicals. A social encyclical is not written in a vacuum. It is the application of timeless truths, derived from natural law and Scripture and developed by theologians, to the problems of a given moment of history. Since social conditions change, concrete papal judgments and warnings may also change, even when they are based on the same enduring moral principles.

It can be said that the papacy has a tendency to "lean against the wind." Knowing that human nature appears to go to extremes, the papacy is often forced to warn against existing trends. Thus, Popes Leo XIII and Pius XI emphasized the need for strong government intervention in economic life, because supine governments in their day permitted grievous exploitation of workers and the politically helpless. As the pendulum swung toward the other extreme, Pope Pius XII warned against unnecessary nationalization of industry and extreme concentration of political power. Faced with a still different set of conditions, it was to be expected that Pope John would come up with answers somewhat at variance with those of his predecessors.

The increasing complexity of social life is a fact. It stems from many factors, such as man's social nature, the growth in population, greater ease of communication, rising living standards, scientific and technical progress, and the ever mounting demands upon the modern state. One need only read about the simpler life of the eighteenth century to realize how all-pervasive is the change today.

Some of this simpler life persisted well into the twentieth century, and the yearning for it shows through in several of the earlier social encyclicals. By contrast, *Mater et Magistra* faces up to modern changes as largely irreversible facts. They have potentialities for good, such as higher living standards, better education, and increased participation in public life. They have their dangers, and the encyclical reflects an awareness of the literature about the organization man, the image makers, and the status seekers. It notes the charge that men are becoming automatons as a result of the pressures of society upon the individual.

But it rejects this charge! What man creates man can control morally. The Pope challenges leaders of government to decentralize power whenever feasible. This is best done by strengthening intermediate groups in society. In terms of our nation, this means revitalizing state and local governments. It calls for giving more power to socially responsible corporations and labor unions. Neighborhood associations should be encouraged to make cities better places in which to live.

This plea for a balance of power, as is clear from the context of both encyclicals, is not the sloganeering "states' rights" of some extremists. These groups oppose federal controls over the economy, but offer no compensating sense of social responsibility on the part of states, corporations, and individuals. Yet government must promote the common good, the general welfare, and it may not remain supinely impotent or inactive when basic human rights are being violated.

THE PURPOSE OF ECONOMIC LIFE

A phrase that recurs throughout both encyclicals is "Economic progress must be accompanied by a corresponding social progress." The Pope rejects the "trickle-down" theory of economic life, which holds that as the economy prospers and accumulates great wealth, much of this will seep down to the poor. This did happen to a degree in some industrial nations, but in others wealth accumulated to the few and destitution remained with the many.

Neither does Pope John accept the Spartan concept, held by most communist nations and some developing countries, that one or two generations must remain in penury while capital is accumulated so that future generations can prosper. Whatever history says about the success of such tactics, the cost in terms of human sacrifice is too great. Economic progress must be matched by increase in social services: education, medical care, good housing, and social insurance. Wealth should be distributed equitably and social inequalities kept to a minimum.

While *Mater et Magistra* does not specify any single method for achieving these goals, it assumes in discussing agriculture that there will be taxation according to ability to pay, social insurance, and government provision for essential social services. The Pope writes in the context of European economies and may be using these examples as illustrations of one method, without indicating that this is necessarily the only feasible way of realizing these ends. The essential point is a fair distribution of national income, eliminating gross disparities between the rich and the poor.

See Social Principles and Economic Life, *Chap. III, especially pp. 38–46 and 54–69.*

Chapter IV

THE SOCIAL VIRTUES

THE COMMON GOOD

Pacem in Terris

53. Individual citizens and intermediate groups are obliged to make their specific contributions to the common welfare. One of the chief consequences of this is that they must bring their own interests into harmony with the needs of the community, and must contribute their goods and their services as civil authorities have prescribed, in accord with the norms of justice and within the limits of their competence. Clearly then those who wield power in the state must do this by such acts which not only have been justly carried out, but which also either have the common welfare primarily in view or which can lead to it.

54. Indeed since the whole reason for the existence of civil authorities is the realization of the common good, it is clearly necessary that, in pursuing this objective, they should respect its essential elements, and at the same time conform their laws to the circumstances of the day.

55. The common good since it is intimately bound up with human nature cannot therefore exist fully and completely unless the human person is taken into consideration and the essential nature and realization of the common good be kept in mind.

56. In the second place, the very nature of the common good requires that all members of the state be entitled to share in it, although in different ways according to each one's tasks, merits, and circumstances. For this reason, every civil authority must take pains to promote the common good of all, without preference for any single citizen or civic group.

Mater et Magistra

78. But a further point needs emphasizing: Any adjustment between wages and profits must take into account the demands of the common good of the particular country and of the whole human family.

79. What are these demands? On the national level they include: employment of the greatest possible number of workers; care lest privileged classes arise, even among the workers; maintenance of equilibrium between wages and prices; the need to make goods and services accessible to the greatest number; elimination, or at least the restriction, of inequalities in the various branches of the economy — that is, between agriculture, industry and services; creation of a proper balance between economic expansion

and the development of social services, especially through the activity of public authorities; the best possible adjustment of the means of production to the progress of science and technology; seeing to it that the benefits which make possible a more human way of life will be available not merely to the present generation but to the coming generations as well.

80. The demands of the common good on the international level include: the avoidance of all forms of unfair competition between the economies of different countries; the fostering of mutual collaboration and good will; and effective co-operation in the development of economically less advanced communities.

SOCIAL JUSTICE

THE encyclical passages excerpted above deal exclusively with the concept of the common good. They are a welcome addition to the material quoted in Chapter IV of *Social Principles and Economic Life*. Many of the earlier excerpts did not define the common good or at most gave rather general indications of its meaning. By contrast, these new selections are much more specific and help us understand what the common good demands when wages and profits are being considered. This point will be treated later as the living wage is discussed. In the present context, these details form a useful supplement to the examples used on pages 75–76 of the above-mentioned text.

Chapter V

CURRENT AND RECENT SOCIAL PHILOSOPHIES

THE SYSTEM OF CAPITALISM

Mater et Magistra

51. It should be stated at the outset that in the economic order first place must be given to the personal initiative of private citizens working either as individuals or in association with each other in various ways for the furtherance of common interests.

52. But — for reasons explained by Our predecessors — the civil power must also have a hand in the economy. It has to promote production in a way best calculated to achieve social progress and the well-being of all citizens.

53. And in this work of directing, stimulating, co-ordinating, supplying and integrating, its guiding principle must be the "principle of subsidiary function" formulated by Pius XI in Quadragesimo Anno.

57. Experience has shown that where personal initiative is lacking, political tyranny ensues and, in addition, economic stagnation in the production of a wide range of consumer goods and of services of the material and spiritual order — those, namely, which are in a great measure dependent upon the exercise and stimulus of individual creative talent.

58. Where, on the other hand, the good offices of the state are lacking or deficient, incurable disorder ensues: in particular, the unscrupulous exploitation of the weak by the strong. For men of this stamp are always in evidence, and, like cockle among the wheat, thrive in every land.

CAPITALISM

THE social writings of the popes rarely use the term *capitalism*. This restraint is necessary because the term means so many different things in various parts of the world. But the passages cited above are an endorsement of the responsible type of capitalism widely advocated and practiced in the United States. They extol individual initiative as the mainspring of economic progress and personal freedom. Yet this personal initiative is not the same as the unlimited right of property as interpreted by the proponents of individualism. An element of government control must also be present both to prevent exploitation and to promote social progress. These points are by no means new developments in Catholic social teaching. But they are noted here to correct certain impressions that the liberal trend in *Mater et Magistra* involved concessions to socialism. Of course, those who define as socialism any government control over business must place in the socialist camp not only Pope John but also his predecessors who wrote on social problems.

See Social Principles and Economic Life, pp. *83–85, 91–93.*

Chapter VI

COMMUNISM

MORAL BASIS OF SOCIETY

Pacem in Terris

34. The dignity of the human person also requires that every man enjoy the right to act freely and responsibly. For this reason, therefore, in social relations man should exercise his rights, fulfill his obligations and, in the countless forms of collaboration with others, act chiefly on his own responsibility and initiative. This is to be done in such a way that each one acts on his own decision, of set purpose and from a consciousness of his obligation, without being moved by force or pressure brought to bear on him externally. For any human society that is established on relations of force must be regarded as inhuman, inasmuch as the personality of its members is repressed or restricted, when in fact they should be provided with appropriate incentives and means for developing and perfecting themselves.

36. Therefore, Venerable Brothers and beloved children, human society must primarily be considered something pertaining to the spiritual. Through it, in the bright light of truth men should share their knowledge, be able to exercise their rights and fulfill their obligations, be inspired to seek spiritual values, mutually derive genuine pleasure from the beautiful of whatever order it be, always be readily disposed to pass on to others the best of their own cultural heritage and eagerly strive to make their own the spiritual achievements of others. These benefits not only influence, but at the same time give aim and scope to all that has bearing on cultural expressions, economic and social institutions, political movements and forms, laws, and all other structures by which society is outwardly established and constantly developed.

37. The order which prevails in society is by nature moral. Grounded as it is in truth, it must function according to the norms of justice, it should be inspired and perfected by mutual love, and finally it should be brought to an ever more refined and human balance in freedom.

48. Wherefore, a civil authority which uses as its only or its chief means either threats and fear of punishment or promises of rewards cannot effectively move men to promote the common good of all. Even if it did so move them, this would be altogether opposed to their dignity as men, endowed with reason and free will. As authority rests chiefly on moral force, it follows that civil authority must appeal primarily to the conscience of individual citizens, that

is, to each one's duty to collaborate readily for the common good of all. But since by nature all men are equal in human dignity, it follows that no one may be coerced to perform interior acts. That is in the power of God alone, who sees and judges the hidden designs of men's hearts.

60. It is agreed that in our time the common good is chiefly guaranteed when personal rights and duties are maintained. The chief concern of civil authorities must therefore be to ensure that these rights are acknowledged, respected, coordinated with other rights, defended and promoted, so that in this way each one may more easily carry out his duties. For *to safeguard the inviolable rights of the human person, and to facilitate the fulfillment of his duties, should be the chief duty of every public authority.*

61. This means that, if any government does not acknowledge the rights of man or violates them, it not only fails in its duty, but its orders completely lack juridical force.

COMMUNIST REGIMES

Pacem in Terris

104. Such expatriations [political refugees] show that there are some political regimes which do not guarantee for individual citizens a sufficient sphere of freedom within which their souls are allowed to breathe humanly; in fact, under those regimes even the lawful existence of such a sphere of freedom is either called into question or denied. This undoubtedly is a radical inversion of the order of human society, because the reason for the existence of public authority is to promote the common good, a fundamental element of which is the recognition of that sphere of freedom and the safeguarding of it.

127. We grant indeed that this conviction [that disputes between nations be resolved through negotiations, not wars] is chiefly based on the terrible destructive force of modern weapons and a fear of the calamities and frightful destruction which such weapons would cause. Therefore, in an age such as ours which prides itself on its atomic energy it is contrary to reason to hold that war is now a suitable way to restore rights which have been violated.

159. It is, therefore, especially to the point to make a clear distinction between false philosophical teachings regarding the nature, origin, and destiny of the universe and of man, and movements which have a direct bearing either on economic and social questions, or cultural matters or on the organization of the state, even if these movements owe their origin and inspiration to these false tenets. While the teaching once it has been clearly set forth is no longer subject to change, the movements, precisely because they take place in the midst of changing conditions, are readily susceptible of change. Besides, who can deny that those movements, in so far as they conform to the dictates of right reason and are interpreters of the lawful aspirations of the human person, contain elements that are positive and deserving of approval?

160. For these reasons it can at times happen that meetings for the attainment of some practical results which previously seemed completely useless now are either actually useful or may be looked upon as profitable for the future. But to decide whether

this moment has arrived, and also to lay down the ways and degrees in which work in common might be possible for the achievement of economic, social, cultural, and political ends which are honorable and useful: these are the problems which can only be solved with the virtue of prudence, which is the guiding light of the virtues that regulate the moral life, both individual and social. Therefore, as far as Catholics are concerned, this decision rests primarily with those who live and work in the specific sectors of human society in which those problems arise, always, however, in accordance with the principles of the natural law, with the social doctrine of the Church, and with the directives of ecclesiastical authorities. For it must not be forgotten that the Church has the right and the duty not only to safeguard the principles of ethics and religion, but also to intervene authoritatively with Her children in the temporal sphere, when there is a question of judging the application of those principles to concrete cases.

OUR discussion of Pope John's views on communism centers exclusively on material taken from *Pacem in Terris*. Only in the final year of his pontificate did he clearly manifest his fresh and somewhat untraditional approach to this problem. The term *communism* is not used in this encyclical, yet it is quite clear that the Pope was deeply concerned with the worldwide impact of militant Marxism.

In contrast to Pope Pius XI, Pope John did not employ any direct denunciations of communist theory or practice. He preferred the positive approach of listing the basic rights necessary for human perfection, orderly society, and world peace. He insisted on man's freedom and the spiritual and moral nature of society and civil authority. Fear is not the proper basis for promoting the common good. A government which denies fundamental rights fails in its duty and indeed lacks the moral right to rule. No Marxist could read the first three parts of this encyclical without being struck by the almost total contrast between the society it portrays and the totalitarian system spawned by Marx and Lenin.

Because communist rule has led to great tyranny, it does not thereby follow that a war of liberation would be just. Indeed, it is "contrary to reason" to hold that in a nuclear age war is a suitable instrument for recovering "rights which have been violated" (No. 127). It is obvious that the direct damage done by nuclear attack, the danger of escalation, and the possibility that we may only be liberating territory rather than people all lessen the desirability of a war of liberation. This principle clearly applies to the nuclear powers. It may also apply in the Orient, if there is reason to believe that the Soviet Union will come to the aid of an ally who has been invaded.

Even phases of the Cold War may well be modified. The sections of the encyclical that seem to apply to this situation (Nos. 159–160) bear on any false philosophical teaching about the nature of man and also on movements based on these same teachings. But in the context of Vatican negotiations with communist powers in 1962 and 1963, it is quite likely that the Pope was here explaining the principles behind this unprecedented policy.

Following this interpretation, we note that atheistic communism is intrinsically evil. But communist movements are subject to change, even though they sprang from Marxist principles and still draw inspiration from them. These movements may have or may develop aspects that conform to the dictates of right reason. They may "contain elements that are positive and deserving of approval."

These observations are not so novel as they appeared to some commentators in early 1963. Pope Pius XI, for all his stringent denunciations of communism, noted that "the communist ideal wins over many of the better-minded members of the community" (*On Atheistic Communism,* No. 15). Moreover, it is a matter of history that communist movements have changed, at least tactically. Soviet and Chinese parties clash bitterly in their interpretation of Marxism, while the Italian communist party insists on its right to an independent line, the so-called polycentrist approach.

Those favoring the exploration of a *détente* with some elements of the communist world may further argue that history shows how the passage of time dulls revolutionary ardor and blunts long-held enmities. Europeans have seen many empires and movements come and go. They expect to see communist movements change as well, as reason, natural law, and conscience prove the falsity of Marxist beliefs. The Iron Curtain can be breached. For centuries religious differences had erected impenetrable barriers in the Christian world, or so it seemed. Yet these "iron curtains" quickly fell, once the ecumenical dialogue was widely accepted.

It is not known how much or how quickly Pope John expected the communist world to change in its attitude toward religion and violent world revolution. Even if the negotiations he initiated prove to be premature, and merely reflect tactical moves by the communist powers, he has given a new approach that may ultimately prove fruitful. The Church can never lessen its opposition to communism as an ideology.

But it can validly take a position as a mediator for peace rather than a partisan in the Cold War.

In the United States, the communist party followed the Kremlin line and began a new policy of friendliness toward religion, especially the Catholic Church. Catholic colleges were invited to accept communist speakers to discuss the encyclical on peace. Catholics were asked to join united-front movements, particularly in connection with peace and race relations. Those who receive these invitations should note the cautious and qualified approach of the encyclical to such ventures. The problem must be faced prudently, by experts, and in conformity to the directives of ecclesiastical authority. Moreover, there is a sharp difference between a dialogue by experts with individual communists who may appear to have good will, and united-front action with a movement that still accepts Marxist ideology and is tightly controlled by the Kremlin.

The communist party in the United States, while weak in comparison to its power and influence during the years 1935–1950, is a potential danger so long as it is an arm of a powerful world revolutionary movement. There is always the chance that social unrest, particularly when fanned by racial tension or unemployment, may create fertile ground for communist growth. Communists may succeed in infiltrating reform groups, such as those seeking racial justice or world peace. The fact that extremists have exaggerated and distorted the menace of domestic subversion should not lead us to forget the potential danger from Leninist tactics of minority seizure of power.

See Social Principles and Economic Life, Chap. VI.

Chapter VII

THE IDEAL SOCIAL ORDER

Mater et Magistra

37. Pius XI saw the re-establishment of the economic world within the framework of the moral order and the subordination of individual and group interests to the interests of the common good as the principal remedies for these evils. This, he taught, necessitated an orderly reconstruction of society, with the establishment of economic and vocational bodies which would be autonomous and independent of the state. Public authority should resume its duty of promoting the common good of all. Finally, there should be co-operation on a world scale for the economic welfare of all nations.

38. Thus Pius XI's teaching in this encyclical can be summed up under two heads. First he taught what the supreme criterion in economic matters ought *not* to be. It must not be the special interests of individuals or groups, nor unregulated competition, economic despotism, national prestige or imperialism, nor any other aim of this sort.

39. On the contrary, all forms of economic enterprise must be governed by the principles of social justice and charity.

40. The second point which We consider basic in the encyclical is his teaching that man's aim must be to achieve in social justice a national and international juridical order, with its network of public and private institutions, in which all economic activity can be conducted not merely for private gain but also in the interests of the common good.

67. So long as social relationships do in fact adhere to these principles within the framework of the moral order, their extension does not necessarily mean that individual citizens will be gravely discriminated against or excessively burdened. On the contrary, we can hope that they will help him to develop and perfect his own personal talents, and lead to that organic reconstruction of society which Our Predecessor Pius XI advocated in his encyclical *Quadragesimo Anno* as the indispensable prerequisite for the fulfillment of the rights and obligations of social life.

WHEN *Mater et Magistra* first appeared newspapers headlined the Pope's alleged turn toward the welfare state. But experts were much more struck by the very brief mention given to the core proposals of *Quadragesimo Anno* for reconstructing economic life, proposals repeatedly endorsed by Pope Pius XII. This basic plan for social reform was summarized accurately in four short paragraphs and then mentioned once more, as a hoped-for outcome of the process of "socialization." Some commentators interpreted this treatment as damning by faint praise. Others felt that the encyclical concentrated on immediate and short-range goals, assuming that long-range plans for social order had been adequately discussed.

The second interpretation appears more plausible. The basic elements of the fundamental social reform advocated in earlier papal writings, as summarized in this encyclical, have permanent validity. Too often, however, impractical commentators used them to build blueprints of a rigid, totally controlled economy. Or they neglected immediate reforms while concentrating upon a distant future. Pope John preferred to emphasize the spirit behind this reform, and he did this by insisting upon social responsibility and the principle of subsidiarity. If these ideals control social-reform movements, they will move in the direction advocated by Pope Pius XI. His goals will be achieved, but in various ways according to the history, temperament, and culture of different national economies. This flexibility was advocated in *Quadragesimo Anno*. Pope John was simply an accurate interpreter of his predecessor.

See Social Principles and Economic Life, *Chap. VII.*

Chapter VIII

RIGHTS AND DUTIES OF CAPITAL

THE RIGHT TO PROFITS

Mater et Magistra

81. These demands of the common good [good faith in productive competition, cooperation in economic affairs, aid to underdeveloped lands], both on a national and a world level, must also be borne in mind when assessing the rate of return due as compensation to the company's management, and as interest or dividends to investors.

DUTIES OF OWNERS

Mater et Magistra

75. We must notice in this connection the system of self-financing adopted in many countries by large, or comparatively large firms. Because these companies are financing replacement and plant expansion out of their own profits, they grow at a very rapid rate. In such cases We believe that the workers should be allocated shares in the firms for which they work, especially when they are paid no more than a minimum wage.

77. Experience suggests many ways in which the demands of justice can be satisfied. Not to mention other ways, it is especially desirable today that workers gradually come to share in the ownership of their company, by ways and in the manner that seem most suitable. For today, even more than in the time of Our Predecessor, "every effort must be made that at least in future a just share only of the fruits of production be permitted to accumulate in the hands of the wealthy, and that an ample sufficiency be supplied to the workers."

CODETERMINATION

Mater et Magistra

91. We, no less than Our predecessors, are convinced that employees are justified in wishing to participate in the activity of the industrial concern for which they work. It is not, of course, possible to lay down hard and fast rules regarding the manner of such participation, for this must depend upon prevailing conditions, which vary from firm to firm and are

frequently subject to rapid and substantial alteration. But We have no doubt as to the need for giving workers an active part in the business of the company for which they work — be it a private or a public one. Every effort must be made to ensure that the enterprise is indeed a true human community, concerned about the needs, the activities, and the standing of each of its members.

92. This demands that the relations between management and employees reflect understanding, appreciation, and good will on both sides. It demands, too, that all parties cooperate actively and loyally in the common enterprise, not so much for what they can get out of it for themselves, but as discharging a duty and rendering a service to their fellow men.

All this implies that the workers have their say in, and make their own contribution to, the efficient running and development of the enterprise. As Pius XII remarked, "the economic and social function which every man aspires to fulfill, demands that the carrying on of the activity of each one is not completely subjected to the others."

Obviously, any firm which is concerned for the human dignity of its workers must also maintain a necessary and efficient unity of direction. But it must not treat those employees who spend their days in service with the firm as though they were mere cogs in the machinery, denying them any opportunity of expressing their wishes or bringing their experience to bear on the work in hand, and keep-ing them entirely passive in regard to decisions that regulate their activity.

93. We would observe, finally, that the present demand for workers to have a greater say in the conduct of the firm accords not only with man's nature, but also with recent progress in the economic, social, and political spheres.

94. For although many unjust and inhuman economic and social imbalances still exist in our day, and there are still many errors affecting the activity, aims, structure, and operation of economies the world over, it is an undeniable fact that, thanks to the driving impulse of scientific and technical advance, productive systems are today rapidly becoming more modernized and efficient— more so than ever before. Hence a greater technical skill is required of the workers, and more exacting professional qualifications. This means that they must be given more assistance, and more free time in which to complete their vocational training as well as to carry out more fittingly their cultural, moral, and religious education.

95. As a further consequence, the modern youth is enabled to devote a longer time to his basic schooling in the arts and sciences.

96. All this serves to create an environment in which workers are encouraged to assume greater responsibility in their own sphere of employment. In politics, too, it is of no small consequence that citizens are becoming daily more aware of their responsibility for furthering the common good in all spheres of life.

PROFITS

WHEN *Mater et Magistra* insists that the monetary return to management, stockholders, and bondholders should be determined by the consideration of the common good, it adopts an approach quite different from that used by some Catholic moralists. Common good involves the virtue of social justice, whereas some writers, such as Monsignor John A. Ryan, discussed these returns only in terms of distributive justice. They concluded that profits could not morally be paid, so long as workers in a plant did not receive a living wage. By contrast, the social-justice approach notes the importance of management incentives provided they satisfy the demands of the common good. Thus it could be argued that failure to give management and investors an adequate return might retard investment, stifle economic growth, and thus hurt labor as well as capital.

The encyclical raises an interesting and often overlooked point when it refers to self-financing of industry. It treats this in a special context, involving a situation in which workers were underpaid in order to build up business capital. Such was the condition in Germany during the years 1949–1957. The stockholders did not contribute this money and should not receive profits from such investments. Instead, workers should be given company stock as a compensation for their sacrifice.

The German form of self-financing is not common here, but another type is rather prevalent. This is financing out of excess profits derived from unduly high prices for company products. Stockholders who received good dividends while this process was going on have no moral claim to the added income derived from such internally financed investments. The first claimant for such returns should be the consumer. He should receive his payment in the form of lower prices or better quality for the same price.

SHARING MANAGEMENT

Pope John goes further than his predecessors in urging business firms to give workers a share in the direction of the company. His approach seems more akin to American human-relations plans than to German codetermination. The Pope upholds unity of management, but asks that workers be considered collaborators and not mere passive recipients of orders. This is not only a demand based on the human dignity of workers, but it is also a special requirement today when workers are better educated and industry requires higher skills.

We might add that plans for sharing in management are often more successful when they are joined with profit-sharing or incentive plans.

This seems to be the basic idea of the well-known Scanlon Plan. It also explains the unexpectedly high returns, at least during the first months of operation, of the complex system adopted by the Kaiser Steel Corporation and the United Steelworkers of America.

See Social Principles and Economic Life, Chap. VIII, pp. 146–161.

Chapter IX

CAPITAL-LABOR RELATIONSHIPS

THE DIGNITY OF LABOR

Mater et Magistra

82. Justice is to be observed not only in the distribution of wealth, but also in regard to the conditions in which men are engaged in producing this wealth. Every man has, of his very nature, a need to express himself in his work and thereby to perfect his own being.

83. Consequently, if the whole structure and organization of an economic system is such as to compromise human dignity, to lessen a man's sense of responsibility or rob him of opportunity for exercising personal initiative, then such a system, We maintain, is altogether unjust — no matter how much wealth it produces, or how justly and equitably such wealth is distributed.

Pacem in Terris

18. If we turn our attention to the economic sphere it is clear that man has a right by the natural law not only to an opportunity to work, but also to go about his work without coercion.

19. To these rights is certainly joined the right to demand working-conditions in which physical health is not endangered, morals are safeguarded, and young people's normal development is not impaired. Women have the right to working conditions in accordance with their requirements and their duties as wives and mothers.

LABOR UNIONS

Mater et Magistra

100. It is Our prerogative to be a Father, and there is a special place in Our thoughts and in Our heart for those professional groups and Christian associations of workers which exist and operate in so many parts of the world. We know the nature and extent of the difficulties under which these dearest sons of Ours are laboring, as they strive continually and effectually to promote in their own countries and throughout the world the material and moral interests of the working people.

101. They are fully deserving of Our praise. The importance of their

work must be gauged not merely by its immediate and obvious results, but also by its effect on the working world as a whole, where it helps to spread sound principles of action and the wholesome influence of the Christian religion.

102. We wish further to praise those dear sons of Ours who in a true Christian spirit collaborate with other professional groups and workers' associations which respect the natural law and the freedom of conscience of their members.

PARTICIPATION IN MANAGEMENT

Mater et Magistra

97. In modern times we have seen an extensive increase in the number of workers' associations, and their general recognition in the juridical codes of single states and on the international level. Members are no longer recruited in order to agitate, but rather to co-operate, principally by the method of collective bargaining. But it is worthwhile stressing here how timely and imperative it is that workers be given the opportunity to exert their influence throughout the state, and not just within the limits of their own spheres of employment.

98. The reason for this is that the individual productive concerns, regardless of their size, efficiency, and importance in the state, form but a part — an integral part — of a nation's entire economic and social life, upon which their own prosperity must depend.

99. Hence it is not the decisions made within the individual productive units which have the greatest bearing on the economy, but those made by public authorities and by institutions which tackle the various economic problems on a national or international basis. It is therefore very appropriate, or even necessary, that these public authorities and institutions bring the workers into their discussions, and those who represent the rights, demands and aspirations of the workingmen; and not confine their deliberations to those who merely represent the interests of management.

HUMAN RELATIONS

POPE JOHN uses strong language when he speaks of the human dignity of the worker. Recognition of this dignity is so essential that an economic system that denied it would be unjust, even though it were otherwise ideal in the production and distribution of wealth. This warning applies to all social systems, but it particularly indicts the communist approach to economic life. Communist leaders have been much more concerned with the quantity of production than with personal initiative or recognition of human dignity.

LABOR UNIONS

There is a largeness of spirit in the encyclical treatment of labor unions.

It is obvious that the Pope trusts organized labor and wishes to enlarge its position in society. He praises Christian and neutral unions alike, notes that members "are no longer recruited to agitate, but rather to co-operate, principally by collective bargaining," and calls for labor participation in bodies that handle "various economic problems on a national or international basis." This is a clear vote of confidence in the aims and competence of union leaders and members.

The Holy See is quite aware that there are voices in the United States that quote papal documents in favor of right-to-work laws and against our religiously neutral union movement. When it became known that a new social encyclical was planned for 1961, these sources sent urgent representations to the Holy See asking that their viewpoint be endorsed in the proposed encyclical. It is not known what action was taken on these proposals. One might infer, however, from the tone of the encyclical, that the Holy See was well pleased with organized labor as a whole. It seemed disposed to leave disputes that might arise in individual countries to the judgment of the bishops of the area.

Those who remember the bitter fight waged against the International Labor Organization by some American management groups note with interest that the Pope expresses "heartfelt appreciation of the work that is being done by the I.L.O." (M.M., No. 103.) More important even than the praise for this particular organization is the implied attitude toward groups working for social reform. Pope John tended to view such activities in perspective. He was not disposed to condemn a noble work because of occasional failures. Nor was he upset by the fact that an international body of necessity had some communists among its members. Those whose spirit is similar to Pope John's instinctively avoid the type of criticism that is purely destructive, niggling, and small-souled.

See Social Principles and Economic Life, Chap. IX, pp. 165–169, 172–173, 177–178, 195–196.

Chapter X

THE LIVING WAGE

FACTORS DETERMINING JUST WAGE

Mater et Magistra

71. We therefore consider it Our duty to reaffirm that the remuneration of work is not something that can be left to the laws of the marketplace; nor should it be a decision left to the will of the more powerful. It must be determined in accordance with justice and equity; which means that workers must be paid a wage which allows them to live a truly human life and to fulfill their family obligations in a worthy manner. Other factors too enter into the assessment of a just wage: namely, the effective contribution which each individual makes to the economic effort, the financial state of the company for which he works, the requirements of the general good of the particular country — having regard especially to the repercussions on the overall employment of the working force in the country as a whole — and finally the requirements of the common good of the universal family of nations of every kind, both large and small.

72. The above principles are valid always and everywhere. So much is clear. But their degree of applicability to concrete cases cannot be determined without reference to the quantity and quality of available resources; and these can — and in fact do — vary from country to country, and even, from time to time, within the same country.

78. But a further point needs emphasizing: Any adjustment between wages and profits must take into account the demands of the common good of the particular country and of the whole human family.

79. What are these demands? On the national level they include: employment of the greatest possible number of workers; care lest privileged classes arise, even among the workers; maintenance of equilibrium between wages and prices; the need to make goods and services accessible to the greatest number; elimination, or at least the restriction, of inequalities in the various branches of the economy — that is, between agriculture, industry, and services; creation of a proper balance between economic expansion and the development of social services, especially through the activity of public authorities; the best possible adjustment of the means of production to the progress of science and technology; seeing to it that the benefits which make possible a more human way of life will be available not merely to the present generation but to the coming generations as well.

HELPING THE LESS DEVELOPED

Mater et Magistra

150. Among citizens of the same political community there is often a marked degree of economic and social inequality. The main reason for this is the fact that they are living and working in different areas, some of which are more economically developed than others.

Where this situation obtains, justice and equity demand that public authority try to eliminate or reduce such imbalances. It should ensure that the less developed areas receive such essential public services as their circumstances require, in order to bring the standard of living in these areas into line with the national average. Furthermore, a suitable economic and social policy must be devised which will take into account the supply of labor, the drift of population, wages, taxes, credit, and the investing of money, especially in expanding industries. In short, it should be a policy designed to promote useful employment, enterprising initiative, and the exploitation of local resources.

151. But the justification of all government action is the common good. Public authority, therefore, must bear in mind the interests of the state as a whole; which means that it must promote all three areas of production — agriculture, industry, and services — simultaneously and evenly. Everything must be done to ensure that citizens of the less developed areas are treated as responsible human beings, and are allowed to play the major role in achieving their own economic, social, and cultural advancement.

152. Private enterprise too must contribute to an economic and social balance in the different areas of the same political community. Indeed, in accordance with "the principle of subsidiary function," public authority must encourage and assist private enterprise, entrusting to it, wherever possible, the continuation of economic development.

Pacem in Terris

32. It is not enough, for example, to acknowledge and respect every man's right to the means of subsistence if we do not strive to the best of our ability for a sufficient supply of what is necessary for his sustenance.

IMPLEMENTING THE LIVING WAGE

POPE JOHN is more explicit than his predecessors in noting the relative nature of a living wage. While the moral claim in terms of human dignity and family needs is absolute, the implementation of this claim depends upon many contingent factors. These include the contribution of the worker himself, the financial health of the company for which he works, and considerations of the national and international common good.

Wage claims must be scrutinized in terms of their effect on employment. Strong bargaining power should not be used to make privileged classes of workers. It should not lead to inflation, economic imbalance, or waste of resources. Wages should not be a factor in unfair international competition, nor should they be a barrier impeding the growth of developing nations.

It would seem that these conditions would be met if wage increases generally did not exceed productivity gains. Even better would be the passing on of such benefits in the form of lower prices, so that all workers would profit by the enhanced value of their weekly pay. This approach would be particularly helpful in redressing inequalities that exist among the sectors of the economy, for example, the low return to agricultural labor in contrast to labor in manufacturing industry. Workers in service occupations are also, as a rule, poorly organized and relatively underpaid.

FULL EMPLOYMENT

National economic policy should be particularly directed toward removing imbalances among agriculture, the services, and industry. The Pope indorses a certain degree of aggressive planning for economic expansion. Such planning, however, must include programs that encourage private enterprise. It should permit citizens of less developed areas to play the major role in achieving their own economic, social, and cultural advancement.

Understandably, the encyclical does not specify which tax, credit, and investment incentive policies are appropriate to achieve these aims. Such details are left to political prudence. They may even require social experimentation and learning by trial and error.

See Social Principles and Economic Life, Chap. X, pp. 198–206, 210–212, 218–223.

Chapter XI

THE ECONOMIC PROBLEMS OF THE FAMILY

Pacem in Terris

41. It is obvious to everyone that women are now taking a part in public life. This is happening more rapidly perhaps in nations of Christian civilization, and, more slowly but broadly, among peoples who have inherited other traditions or cultures. Since women are becoming ever more conscious of their human dignity, they will not tolerate being treated as mere material instruments, but demand rights befitting a human person both in domestic and in public life.

WOMEN WORKERS

IT IS a happy characteristic of modern life that the rights and the human dignity of women are more universally respected. One illustration of this fact was the enactment by the United States Congress, almost at the time of the issuance of the peace encyclical, of a law guaranteeing to women pay equal to that given to men for similar work. During the same year a White House Committee issued a study calling for greater utilization of women's skills in the economy.

In the past, Catholic writers almost universally deplored the unnecessary employment of women outside the home. However, there is now a growing minority that maintains that outside work need not hurt family life, even when children are small. The argument states that a mother using her talents more fully is more content, happier, and hence a better parent. Again, women should ponder deeply the responsibilities of marriage and parenthood, intelligently and creatively seeking ways to utilize their talents and education in the sphere of domestic activity.

See Social Principles and Economic Life, Chap. XI, pp. 225–226, 241–243.

Chapter XII

PROPERTY

PROPERTY IN MODERN LIFE

Mater et Magistra

43. Concerning the use of material goods, Our Predecessor declared that the right of every man to use these for his own sustenance is prior to every other economic right, even that of private property. The right to the private possession of material goods is admittedly a natural one; nevertheless, in the objective order established by God, the right to property cannot stand in the way of the axiomatic principle that "the goods which were created by God for all men should flow to all alike, according to the principles of justice and charity."

104. It is well known that in recent years in the larger industrial concerns a distinction has been growing between the ownership of productive goods and the responsibility of company managers. This has created considerable problems for public authorities, whose duty it is to see that the aims pursued by the leaders of the principal organizations — especially those which have an important part to play in the national economy — do not conflict in any way with the interests of the common good. Experience shows that these problems arise whether the capital which makes possible these vast undertakings belongs to private citizens or to public corporations.

105. It is also true that more and more people today, through belonging to insurance groups and systems of social security, find that they can face the future with confidence — the sort of confidence which formerly resulted from their possession of a certain amount of property.

106. And another thing happening today is that people are aiming at proficiency in their trade or profession rather than the acquisition of private property. They think more highly of an income which derives from work and the rights consequent upon work, than of an income which derives from capital and the rights of capital.

107. And this as it should be. Work, which is the immediate expression of a human personality, must always be rated higher than the possession of external goods which of their very nature are merely instrumental. This view of work is certainly an indication of an advance that has been made in our civilization.

Confirmation of the right of ownership

108. What, then, of that social and economic principle so vigorously asserted and defended by Our predecessors: man's natural right to own

private property, including productive goods? Is this no longer operative today, or has it lost some of its validity in view of the economic conditions We have described above? This is the doubt that has arisen in many minds.

109. There is no reason for such a doubt to persist. The right of private ownership of goods, including productive goods, has permanent validity. It is part of the natural order, which teaches that the individual is prior to society and that society must be ordered to the good of the individual.

Moreover, it would be quite useless to insist on free and personal initiative in the economic field, while at the same time withdrawing man's right to dispose freely of the means indispensable to the achievement of such initiative.

Further, history and experience testify that in those political regimes which do not recognize the rights of private ownership of goods, productive included, the exercise of freedom in almost every other direction is suppressed or stifled. This suggests, surely, that the exercise of freedom finds its guarantee and incentive in the right of ownership.

110. This explains why social and political movements for the harmonizing of justice and freedom in society, though until recently opposed to the private ownership of productive goods, are today reconsidering their position in the light of a clearer understanding of social history, and are in fact now declaring themselves in favor of this right.

Always vast field for personal charity

120. In recent years the state and other agencies of public law have extended, and are continuing to extend, the sphere of their activity and initiative. But this does not mean that the doctrine of the social function of private ownership is out of date, as some would maintain. It is inherent in the very right of private ownership.

Then, too, a further consideration arises. Tragic situations and urgent problems of an intimate and personal nature are continually arising which the state with all its machinery is unable to remedy or assist. There will always remain, therefore, a vast field for the exercise of human sympathy and the Christian charity of individuals. We would observe, finally, that the efforts of individuals or of groups of private citizens, are definitely more effective in promoting spiritual values than is the activity of public authority.

TAXATION

Mater et Magistra

132. In a system of taxation based on justice and equity it is fundamental that the burdens be proportioned to the capacity of the people contributing.

A JUST DISTRIBUTION OF PROPERTY

Mater et Magistra

84. It is not possible to give a concise definition of the kind of economic structure which is most consonant with man's dignity and best calculated to develop in him a sense of responsibility. Pius XII, however,

comes to our rescue with the following directive: "The small and average sized undertakings in agriculture, in the arts and crafts, in commerce and industry, should be safeguarded and fostered. Moreover, they should join together in co-operative associations to gain for themselves the benefits and advantages that usually can be gained only from large organizations. In the large concerns themselves there should be the possibility of moderating the contract of work by one of partnership."

85. Hence the craftsman's business and that of the family farm, as well as the co-operative enterprise which aims at the completion and perfection of both these concerns — all these are to be safeguarded and encouraged in harmony with the common good and technical progress.

86. We shall return shortly to the question of the family farm. Here We consider it appropriate to say something about artisan and co-operative enterprises.

87. First of all it is necessary to emphasize that if these two kinds of undertaking are to thrive and prosper they must be prepared constantly to adjust their productive equipment and their productive methods to meet new situations created by the advance of science and technology and the changing demands and preferences of the consumer. This adaptation must be effected principally by the workers themselves and the members of the co-operatives.

88. Both these groups, therefore, need a thoroughgoing technical and general education, and should have their own professional organizations. It is equally important that the government take the proper steps regarding their training, taxation, credit, social security, and insurance.

89. Furthermore, these two categories of citizens — craftsmen and members of co-operatives — are fully entitled to these watchful measures of the state, for they are upholding true human values and contributing to the advance of civilization.

90. We therefore paternally invite Our beloved sons — craftsmen and members of co-operatives throughout the world — to realize the greatness of this task which is theirs in the state. By the force of their example they are helping to keep alive in their own community a true sense of responsibility, a spirit of co-operation, and the constant desire to create new and original work of outstanding merit.

115. Now, if ever, is the time to insist on a more widespread distribution of property, in view of the rapid economic development of an increasing number of states. It will not be difficult for the body politic, by the adoption of various techniques of proved efficiency, to pursue an economic and social policy which facilitates the widest possible distribution of private property in terms of durable consumer goods, houses, land, tools and equipment (in the case of craftsmen and owners of family farms), and shares in medium and large business concerns. This policy is in fact being pursued with considerable success by several of the socially and economically advanced nations.

THE RIGHT TO PRIVATE PROPERTY

REPORTEDLY, the section on private property caused considerable controversy during the preparation of the encyclical *Mater et Magistra*. It has been asserted that debate over its provisions held up the issuance of the document for two months. If these assertions are factual, only traces of the debate can be found in the final version. Even the startling, to some, statement that the right to use goods for one's sustenance is prior to the right of private property is by no means novel, since it comes from St. Thomas Aquinas. A starving man may take food and not be guilty of the sin of theft.

Separation of ownership and control in the large corporation is noted in the encyclical and there is some mention of the problems that this creates. But this fact is not used to make important modifications in the traditional doctrine on private property, as some European thinkers desired. Also noted is the fact that today social security, pensions, and work skills give to many people the personal security that men formerly sought from property ownership. This point has been well developed in articles written by Rev. Edward Duff, S.J. But the Holy See is not prepared to accept these developments as supplanting private property in some of its age-old functions. Instead the Pope repeats the position that property rights not only give security to individuals, but also constitute a necessary basis for political freedom. He indicates that even the socialists are changing to this point of view.

Although government is extending its functions today, there still remains a most important sphere for private use of property. There are tragic situations and personal problems which the state cannot touch. Accordingly there will always remain a vast field for the exercise of human sympathy and personal charity. This point is extremely important today, as the depersonalization of society leaves many persons be-wildered and even disoriented.

A WIDER DIFFUSION OF OWNERSHIP

Private property will fulfill its historic functions only if it is widely distributed. Pope John made more specific this position of the social popes by listing types of property that should be distributed: durable consumer goods; houses; land; tools and equipment for craftsmen, small business, and family farms; and shares of stock in medium and large business concerns.

The encyclical repeats the directive of Pope Pius XII that small business and crafts should be fostered and safeguarded. Once again, however, it is practical and down-to-earth. These activities must be modernized if they are to survive. They should form co-operatives. Their owners should have a thorough general and technical education. Government should aid them in matters involving taxation, credit, social security, and insurance. They are entitled to this special protection because of their contribution to the advance of civilization.

If democracy is to flourish, there must be many persons in a community who possess the economic basis of freedom. This derives from personal ownership of productive property. Such owners secure their incomes without close dependence upon the state or the large corporation. Neither the welfare state nor the beneficent corporation can confer the independence and security that derives from the ownership of a small business or family farm or the practice of a skilled craft as a contractor-worker.

See *Social Principles and Economic Life, Chap. XII, pp. 250–252, 255–262, 268–275.*

Chapter XIII

THE STATE IN ECONOMIC LIFE

PUBLIC AUTHORITY

Pacem in Terris

67. It is impossible to determine, in all cases, what is the most suitable form of government, or how civil authorities can most effectively fulfill their respective functions, i.e., the legislative, judicial, and executive functions of the state.

68. In determining the structure and operation of government which a state is to have, great weight has to be given to the circumstances of a given people, circumstances which will vary at different times and in different places. We consider, however, that it is in keeping with the innate demands of human nature that the state should take a form which embodies the threefold division of powers corresponding to the three principal functions of public authority. In that type of state, not only the official functions of government but also the mutual relations between citizens and public officials are set down according to law, which in itself affords protection to the citizens both in the enjoyment of their rights and in the fulfillment of their duties.

69. If, however, this political and juridical structure is to produce the advantages which may be expected of it, public officials must strive to meet the problems which arise in a way that conforms both to the complexities of the situation and the proper exercise of their function. This requires that, in constantly changing conditions, legislators never forget the norms of morality, or constitutional provisions, or the common good. Moreover, executive authorities must co-ordinate the activities of society with discretion, with a full knowledge of the law and after a careful consideration of circumstances, and the courts must administer justice impartially and without being influenced by favoritism or pressure. The good order of society also demands that individual citizens and intermediate organizations should be effectively protected by law whenever they have rights to be exercised or obligations to be fulfilled. This protection should be granted to citizens both in their dealings with each other and in their relations with government agencies.

75. From these considerations it becomes clear that in the juridical organization of states in our times the first requisite is that a charter of fundamental human rights be drawn up in clear and precise terms and that it be incorporated in its entirety in the constitution.

76. The second requisite is that

the constitution of each state be drawn up, phrased in correct juridical terminology, which prescribes the manner of designating the public officials along with their mutual relations, the spheres of their competence, the forms and systems they are obliged to follow in the performance of their office.

77. The last requisite is that the relations between the government and the governed are then set forth in terms of rights and duties; and it is clearly laid down that the paramount task assigned to government officials is that of recognizing, respecting, reconciling, protecting, and promoting the rights and duties of citizens.

DUTIES OF CITIZENS

Pacem in Terris

26. The dignity of the human person involves the right to take an active part in public affairs and to contribute one's part to the common good of the citizens. For, as Our Predecessor of happy memory, Pius XII, pointed out: *The human individual, far from being an object and, as it were, a merely passive element in the social order, is, in fact, must be and must continue to be, its subject, its foundation and its end.*

27. The human person is also entitled to a juridical protection of his rights, a protection that should be efficacious, impartial, and inspired by the true norms of justice. As Our Predecessor Pius XII teaches: *That perpetual privilege proper to man, by which every individual has a claim to the protection of his rights, and by which there is assigned to each a definite and particular sphere of rights, immune from all arbitrary attacks, is the logical consequence of the order of justice willed by God.*

73. It is in keeping with their dignity as persons that human beings should take an active part in government, although the manner in which they share in it will depend on the level of development of the country to which they belong.

74. Men will find new and extensive advantages in the fact that they are allowed to participate in government. In this situation, those who administer the government come into frequent contact with the citizens, and it is thus easier for them to learn what is really needed for the common good. And since public officials hold office only for a specified period of time their authority, far from withering, rather takes on a new vigor in a measure proportionate to the development of human society.

146. Once again We exhort Our children to take an active part in public life, and to contribute toward the attainment of the common good of the entire human family as well as to that of their own country. They should endeavor, therefore, in the light of the Faith and with the strength of love, to ensure that the various institutions — whether economic, social, cultural, or political in purpose — should be such as not to create obstacles, but rather to facilitate or render less arduous man's perfectioning of himself both in the natural order as well as in the supernatural.

SOCIAL LEGISLATION

Mater et Magistra

20. As for the state, its whole raison d'être is the realization of the common good in the temporal order. It cannot, therefore, hold aloof from economic matters. On the contrary, it must do all in its power to promote the production of a sufficient supply of material goods, "the use of which is necessary for the practice of virtue." It has also the duty to protect the rights of all its people, and particularly of its weaker members, the workers, women and children. It can never be right for the state to shirk its obligation of working actively for the betterment of the condition of the workingman.

21. It is furthermore the duty of the state to ensure that terms of employment are regulated in accordance with justice and equity, and to safeguard the human dignity of workers by making sure that they are not required to work in an environment which may prove harmful to their material and spiritual interests.

54. The present advance in scientific knowledge and productive technology clearly puts it within the power of the public authority to a much greater degree than ever before to reduce imbalances which may exist between different branches of the economy or between different regions within the same country or even between the different peoples of the world. It also puts into the hands of public authority a greater means for limiting fluctuations in the economy and for providing effective measures to prevent the recurrence of mass unemployment. Hence the insistent demands on those in authority — since they are responsible for the common good — to increase the degree and scope of their activities in the economic sphere, and to devise ways and means and set the necessary machinery in motion for the attainment of this end.

55. But however extensive and far-reaching the influence of the state on the economy may be, it must never be exerted to the extent of depriving the individual citizen of his freedom of action. It must rather augment his freedom while effectively guaranteeing the protection of his essential personal rights. Among these is a man's right and duty to be primarily responsible for his own upkeep and that of his family. Hence every economic system must permit and facilitate the free development of productive activity.

56. Moreover, as history itself testifies with ever increasing clarity, there can be no such thing as a well-ordered and prosperous society unless individual citizens and the state co-operate in the economy. Both sides must work together in harmony, and their respective efforts must be proportioned to the needs of the common good in the prevailing circumstances and conditions of human life.*

* See also excerpts cited in Chapter V.

Pacem in Terris

56. Considerations of justice and equity, however, can at times demand that those involved in civil government give more attention to the less fortunate members of the community, since they are less able to defend their rights and to assert their legitimate claims.

57. In this context, We judge that attention should be called to the fact that the common good touches the whole man, the needs both of his body and of his soul. Hence it follows that the civil authorities must undertake to effect the common good by ways and means that are proper to them; that is, while respecting the hierarchy of values, they should promote simultaneously both the material and the spiritual welfare of the citizens.

63. It is also demanded by the common good that civil authorities

Duty of promoting the rights of individuals

should make earnest efforts to bring about a situation in which individual citizens can easily exercise their rights and fulfill their duties as well. For experience has taught us that, unless these authorities take suitable action with regard to economic, political, and cultural matters, inequalities between the citizens tend to become more and more widespread, especially in the modern world, and as a result human rights are rendered totally ineffective and the fulfillment of duties is compromised.

64. It is therefore necessary that the administration give wholehearted and careful attention to the social as well as to the economic progress of the citizens, and to the development, in keeping with the development of the productive system, of such essential services as the building of roads, transportation, communications, water supply, housing, public health, education, facilitation of the practice of religion, and recreational facilities. It is necessary also that governments make efforts to see that insurance systems are made available to the citizens, so that, in case of misfortune or increased family responsibilities, no person will be without the necessary means to maintain a decent standard of living. The government should make similarly effective efforts to see that those who are able to work can find employment in keeping with their aptitudes, and that each worker receives a wage in keeping with the laws of justice and equity. It should be equally the concern of civil authorities to ensure that workers be allowed their proper responsibility in the work undertaken in industrial organization, and to facilitate the establishment of intermediate groups which will make social life richer and more effective. Finally, it should be possible for all the citizens to share as far as they are able in their country's cultural advantages.

CIVIL AUTHORITY

SO RICH was the pontificate of Pope John XXIII that many eulogists overlooked one of his major contributions, namely, his placing of the Catholic Church unequivocally on the side of democracy. *Pacem in Terris* should finally lay to rest the controversies and ambiguities stemming from papal reaction to the new democracies in the confused circumstances of the nineteenth century. It is true that Pope Pius XII eulogized the democratic form of government in his Christmas message of 1944. But Pope John's encyclical on peace is specific, precise, and unreserved in its acceptance of the modern democracy.

Necessarily the encyclical states that one cannot determine once and for all the most suitable form of government. Traditionally the Church has remained neutral in regard to various types of political organization, asking only that rulers act justly and according to law. But the present encyclical clearly implies that democracy is the best form of government. It "is in keeping with the innate demands of human nature" that there should be a threefold division of powers: legislative, executive, and judicial. The state should have a charter or constitution that spells out the human rights of the citizens and specifies the precise powers and duties of the different branches of government. Authority should be exercised according to law and with full respect for the rights and duties of citizens. Ministers of government should hold office only for a limited time.

Although the Church has recognized the legitimacy of various forms of government, it is proper to note that participation in public affairs is a right that stems from the dignity of the human person. Indeed, it is not merely a right, it is also a duty. It is true that the extent of participation will depend upon the level of development of a country. Yet those who exercise absolute rule over citizens, whether as king, dictator, or aristocrat, should prepare their subjects to participate in political life so that eventually they may rule themselves.

GOVERNMENT IN ECONOMIC LIFE

Both social encyclicals of Pope John spell out the rights and duties of the state in regard to economic life. The earlier encyclical gives an excellent summary of previous papal teachings in this area. It then notes two specific functions which are of the highest importance today. These are reducing imbalances among various regions and sectors of the economy, and the smoothing of the business cycle together with the prevention of mass unemployment. Public authority is better able today, because of advances in economic knowledge and gains in technical achievement, to secure these results. Consequently, the duty of government to promote the common good calls for effective action in these spheres. But this authority should not be exercised in an autocratic way. The state should protect the personal rights of citizens. Both the citizen and the state should co-operate and work in harmony, in a manner indicated by the present needs of the common good.

Pacem in Terris puts particular stress on the duty of government to reduce inequalities in regard to economic, political, and cultural affairs. Social progress should be given equal priority with economic progress. Essential public services should be available to all citizens. Government should see that the people have adequate social insurance, not only to cover misfortunes, but also to aid when family responsibilities are increased. Suitable employment and just wages should be available to all. However, it does not necessarily follow that each of these advantages should be directly provided by the state. When the state fosters the development of intermediate groups, these "will make social life richer and more effective."

It would not be accurate to call these directives a plea for the welfare state. Nothing is stated here that was not advocated in principle in the social encyclicals of recent popes. Where Pope John is different is largely in the specific nature of his examples. These illustrations embody many features that some conservatives characterize as part of the welfare state. But the precise genius of Pope John is his encouragement of citizens to preserve traditional values of initiative and independence, while recognizing that the complexity of modern society involves necessarily a greater degree of social control than was required in the nineteenth century. He does not fight developments, he only asks that they be kept in proper balance.

Whether or not this is a "shift to the left" is largely a matter of semantics. Pope John emphasizes individual initiative and the principle of subsidiarity, but he does this in the context of the modern world. He accepts the complexity of modern society, and the consequent increase of influences and controls affecting the individual, as an accomplished fact. But he does not hold that these trends, of necessity, must compromise basic freedoms or prevent adequate decentralization of power.

See Social Principles and Economic Life, Chap. XIII, pp. 276–281, 283–289. 292–295.

Chapter XIV

INTERNATIONAL POLITICAL AND ECONOMIC LIFE

INTERDEPENDENCE OF NATIONS

Mater et Magistra

200. The progress of science and technology in every aspect of life has led, particularly today, to increased relationships between nations, and made the nations more and more dependent on one another.

201. As a rule no single commonwealth has sufficient resources at its command to solve the more important scientific, technical, economic, social, political, and cultural problems which confront it at the present time. These problems are necessarily the concern of a whole group of nations, and possibly of the whole world.

202. Individual political commu-nities may indeed enjoy a high degree of culture and civilization. They may have a large and industrious population, an advanced economic structure, great natural resources and extensive territories. Yet, even so, in isolation from the rest of the world they are quite incapable of finding an adequate solution to their major problems. The nations, therefore, must work with each other for their mutual development and perfection. They can help themselves only in so far as they succeed in helping one another. That is why international understanding and co-operation are so necessary.

Pacem in Terris

88. Likewise it can happen that one country surpasses another in scientific progress, culture, and economic development. But this superiority, far from permitting it to rule others unjustly, imposes the obligation to make a greater contribution to the general development of the people.

91. Relations between nations are to be further regulated by justice. This implies, over and above recognition of their mutual rights, the fulfillment of their respective duties.

92. Since nations have a right to exist, to develop themselves, to acquire a supply of the resources necessary for their development, to defend their good name and the honor due to them, it follows that they are likewise bound by the obligation of effectively guarding each of these rights and of avoiding those actions by which these rights can be jeopardized. As men in their private enterprises cannot pursue their own interests to the detriment of others, so too states cannot lawfully seek that

development of their own resources which brings harm to other states and unjustly oppresses them.

98. Since the mutual relations among nations must be regulated by the norm of truth and justice, they must also derive great advantage from an energetic union of mind, heart, and resources. This can be effected at various levels by mutual co-operation in many ways, as is happening in our own time with beneficial results in the economic, social, political, educational, public health, and sports spheres. We must remember that, of its very nature, civil authority exists, not to confine its people within the boundaries of their nation, but rather to protect, above all else, the common good of that particular civil society, which certainly cannot be divorced from the common good of the entire human family.

99. So it happens that civil societies in pursuing their interests not only must not harm others, but must join their plans and forces whenever the efforts of an individual government cannot achieve its desired goals; but in the execution of such common efforts, great care must be taken lest what helps some nations should injure others.

118. In the highest and most authoritative assemblies, let men give serious thought to the problem of a peaceful adjustment of relations between political communities on a world level: an adjustment founded on mutual trust, on sincerity in negotiations, on faithful fulfillment of obligations assumed. Let them study the problem until they find that point of agreement from which it will be possible to commence to go forward toward accords that will be sincere, lasting, and fruitful.

130. The recent progress of science and technology, since it has profoundly influenced human conduct, is rousing men everywhere in the world to more and more co-operation and association with one another. Today the exchange of goods and ideas, travel from one country to another have greatly increased. Consequently, the close relations of individuals, families, intermediate associations belonging to different countries have become vastly more frequent and conferences between heads of states are held at shorter intervals. At the same time the interdependence of national economies has grown deeper, one becoming progressively more closely related to the other, so that they become, as it were, integral parts of the one world economy. Finally, the social progress, order, security, and peace of each country are necessarily connected with the social progress, order, security, and peace of all other countries.

131. Given these conditions, it is obvious that individual countries cannot rightly seek their own interests and develop themselves in isolation from the rest, for the prosperity and development of one country follows partly in the train of the prosperity and progress of all the rest and partly produces that prosperity and progress.

A universal public authority

137. Today the universal common good poses problems of world-wide dimensions, which cannot be adequately tackled or solved except by the efforts of public authority endowed with a wideness of powers, structure and means of the same proportions: that is, of public authority which is in a position to operate in an effective manner on a world-wide basis. The moral order itself, therefore, demands that such a form of public authority be established.

138. This public authority, having world-wide power and endowed with the proper means for the efficacious

pursuit of its objective, which is the universal common good in concrete form, must be set up by common accord and not imposed by force. The reason is that such an authority must be in a position to operate effectively; yet, at the same time, its action must be inspired by sincere and real impartiality: It must be an action aimed at satisfying the universal common good. The difficulty is that there would be reason to fear that a supranational or world-wide public authority, imposed by force by the more powerful nations, might be an instrument of one-sided interests; and even should this not happen, it would be difficult for it to avoid all suspicion of partiality in its actions, and this would take from the force and effectiveness of its activity. Even though there may be pronounced differences between nations as regards the degree of their economic development and their military power, they are all very sensitive as regards their juridical equality and the excellence of their way of life. For that reason, they are right in not easily yielding obedience to an authority imposed by force, or to an authority in whose creation they had no part, or to which they themselves did not decide to submit by their own free choice.

The universal common good and personal rights

139. Like the common good of individual states, so too the universal common good cannot be determined except by having regard for the human person. Therefore, the public and universal authority, too, must

have as its fundamental objective the recognition, respect, safeguarding and promotion of the rights of the human person; this can be done by direct action when required, or by creating on a world scale an environment in which leaders of the individual countries can suitably maintain their own functions.

140. Moreover, just as it is necessary in each state that relations which the public authority has with its citizens, families, and intermediate associations be controlled and regulated by the principle of subsidiarity, it is equally necessary that the relationships which exist between the world-wide public authority and the public authorities of individual nations be governed by the same principle. This means that the world-wide public authority must tackle and solve problems of an economic, social, political, or cultural character which are posed by the universal common good. For, because of the vastness, complexity, and urgency of those problems, the public authorities of the individual states are not in a position to tackle them with any hope of a positive solution.

141. The world-wide public authority is not intended to limit the sphere of action of the public authority of the individual state, much less to take its place. On the contrary, its purpose is to create, on a world basis, an environment in which the public authorities of each state, its citizens and intermediate associations, can carry out their tasks, fulfill their duties and exercise their rights with greater security.

POPULATION PROBLEMS

Mater et Magistra

185. How can economic development and the supply of food keep pace with the continual rise in population? This is a question which

constantly obtrudes itself today — a world problem, as well as one for the poverty-stricken nations.

186. As a world problem, the case is put thus: According to sufficiently reliable statistics the next few decades will see a very great increase in human population, whereas economic development will proceed at a slower rate. Hence, we are told, if nothing is done to check this rise in population, the world will be faced in the not too distant future with an increasing shortage in the necessities of life.

187. As it affects the less developed countries, the problem is stated thus: The resources of modern hygiene and medicine will very shortly bring about a notable decrease in the mortality rate, especially among infants, while the birth rate — which in such countries is usually high — will tend to remain more or less constant, at least for a considerable period. The excess of births over deaths will therefore show a steep rise, whereas there will be no corresponding increase in the productive efficiency of the economy. Accordingly, the standard of living in these poorer countries cannot possibly improve. It must surely worsen, even to the point of extreme hardship. Hence there are those who hold the opinion that, in order to prevent a serious crisis from developing, the conception and birth of children should be secretly avoided, or in any event, curbed in some way.

188. Truth to tell, we do not seem to be faced with any immediate or imminent world problem arising from the disproportion between the increase of population and the supply of food. Arguments to this effect are based on such unreliable and controversial data that they can only be of very uncertain validity.

189. Besides, the resources which God in His goodness and wisdom has implanted in Nature are well-nigh inexhaustible, and He has at the same time given man the intelligence to discover ways and means of exploiting these resources for his own advantage and his own livelihood. Hence, the real solution of the problem is not to be found in expedients which offend against the divinely established moral order and which attack human life at its very source, but in a renewed scientific and technical effort on man's part to deepen and extend his dominion over Nature. The progress of science and technology that has already been achieved opens up almost limitless horizons in this field.

190. As for the problems which face the poorer nations in various parts of the world, We realize, of course, that these are very real. They are caused, more often than not, by a deficient economic and social organization, which does not offer living conditions proportionate to the increase in population. They are caused, also, by the lack of effective solidarity among such peoples.

191. But granting this, We must nevertheless state most emphatically that no statement of the problem and no solution to it is acceptable which does violence to man's essential dignity; those who propose such solutions base them on an utterly materialistic conception of man himself and his life.

Only possible solution

192. The only possible solution to this question is one which envisages the social and economic progress both of individuals and of the whole of human society, and which respects and promotes true human values. First consideration must obviously be given to those values which concern man's dignity generally, and the immense worth of each individual human life. Attention must then be turned to

the need for worldwide co-operation among men, with a view to a fruitful and well-regulated interchange of useful knowledge, capital, and manpower.

199. A provident God grants sufficient means to the human race to find a dignified solution to the problems attendant upon the transmission of human life. But these problems can become difficult of solution, or even insoluble, if man, led astray in mind and perverted in will, turns to such means as are opposed to right reason, and seeks ends that are contrary to his social nature and the intentions of Providence.

INTERNATIONAL ECONOMIC PROBLEMS

Mater et Magistra

80. The demands of the common good on the international level include: the avoidance of all forms of unfair competition between the economies of different countries; the fostering of mutual collaboration and good will; and effective co-operation in the development of economically less advanced communities.

153. It is not out of place to remark here on a problem which exists in quite a number of countries, namely, a gross disproportion between land and population. In some countries arable land abounds, but there is a scarcity of population; whereas in other countries the position is reversed: the population is large, arable land scarce.

154. Again, some countries use primitive methods of agriculture, with the result that, for all their abundance of natural resources, they are not able to produce enough food to feed their population; whereas other countries, using modern methods of agriculture, produce a surplus of food which has an adverse effect on the economy.

155. It is therefore obvious that the solidarity of the human race and Christian brotherhood demand the elimination as far as possible of these discrepancies. With this object in view, people all over the world must co-operate actively with one another in all sorts of ways, so as to facilitate the movement of goods, capital, and men from one country to another. We shall have more to say on this point later on.

156. Here We would like to express Our sincere appreciation of the work which the F.A.O. has undertaken to establish effective collaboration among nations, to promote the modernization of agriculture especially in less developed countries, and to alleviate the suffering of hunger-stricken peoples.

Obligation of the wealthy nations

157. Probably the most difficult problem today concerns the relationship between political communities that are economically advanced and those in the process of development. Whereas the standard of living is high in the former, the latter are subject to extreme poverty. The solidarity which binds all men together as members of a common family makes it impossible for wealthy nations to look with indifference upon the hunger, misery and poverty of other nations whose citizens are unable to enjoy even elementary human rights. The nations of the world are becoming more and more dependent on one another and it will not be possible to preserve a lasting peace so long as glaring economic and social imbalances persist.

158. Mindful of Our position as

the father of all peoples, We feel constrained to repeat here what We said on another occasion: "We are all equally responsible for the under-nourished peoples. [Hence], it is necessary to educate one's conscience to the sense of responsibility which weighs upon each and every one, especially upon those who are more blessed with this world's goods."

160. It is therefore a great source of joy to Us to see those nations which enjoy a high degree of economic wealth helping the nations not so well provided, so that they may more effectively raise their standard of living.

161. Justice and humanity demand that those countries which produce consumer goods, especially farm products, in excess of their own needs should come to the assistance of those other countries where large sections of the population are suffering from want and hunger. It is nothing less than an outrage to justice and humanity to destroy or to squander goods that other people need for their very lives.

162. We are, of course, well aware that overproduction, especially in agriculture, can cause economic harm to a certain section of the population. But it does not follow that one is thereby exonerated from extending emergency aid to those who need it. On the contrary, everything must be done to minimize the ill effects of overproduction, and to spread the burden equitably over the entire population.

Scientific, technical, and financial co-operation

163. Of itself, however, emergency aid will not go far in relieving want and famine when these are caused — as they so often are — by the primitive state of a nation's economy. The only permanent remedy for this is to make use of every possible means of providing these citizens with the scientific, technical, and professional training they need, and to put at their disposal the necessary capital for speeding up their economic development with the help of modern methods.

164. We are aware how deeply the public conscience has been affected in recent years by the urgent need of supporting the economic development and social progress of those countries which are still struggling against poverty and economic disabilities.

165. International and regional organizations, national and private societies, all are working toward this goal, increasing day by day the measure of their own technical co-operation in all productive spheres. By their combined efforts thousands of young people are being given facilities for attending the universities of the more advanced countries, and acquiring an up-to-date scientific, technical, and professional training. World banking institutes, individual states and private persons are helping to furnish the capital for an ever richer network of economic enterprises in the less wealthy countries. It is a magnificent work that they are doing, and We are most happy to take this occasion of giving it the praise that it deserves. It is a work, however, which needs to be increased, and We hope that the years ahead will see the wealthier nations making even greater efforts for the scientific, technical, and economic advancement of those political communities whose development is still only in its initial stages.

166. We consider it Our duty to give further advice on this matter.

Learning from other nations

167. In the first place, those nations which are still only at the be-

ginning of their journey along the road to economic development would do well to consider carefully the experiences of the wealthier nations which have traversed this road before them.

168. Increase in production and productive efficiency is, of course, sound policy, and indeed a vital necessity. However, it is no less necessary — and justice itself demands — that the riches produced be distributed fairly among all members of the political community. This means that everything must be done to ensure that social progress keeps pace with economic progress. Again, every sector of the economy — agriculture, industry and the services — must progress evenly and simultaneously.

169. The developing nations, obviously, have certain unmistakable characteristics of their own, resulting from the nature of the particular region and the natural dispositions of their citizens, with their time-honored traditions and customs.

170. In helping these nations, therefore, the more advanced communities must recognize and respect this individuality. They must beware of making the assistance they give an excuse for forcing these people into their own national mold.

Offering disinterested aid

171. There is also a further temptation which the economically developed nations must resist: that of giving technical and financial aid with a view to gaining control over the political situation in the poorer countries, and furthering their own plans for world domination.

172. Let us be quite clear on this point. A nation that acted from these motives would in fact be introducing a new form of colonialism — cleverly disguised, no doubt, but actually reflecting that older, outdated type from which many nations have recently emerged. Such action would, moreover, have a harmful impact on international relations, and constitute a menace to world peace.

173. Necessity, therefore, and justice demand that all such technical and financial aid be given without thought of domination, but rather for the purpose of helping the less developed nations to achieve their own economic and social growth.

174. If this can be achieved, then a precious contribution will have been made to the formation of a world community, in which each individual nation, conscious of its rights and duties, can work on terms of equality with the rest for the attainment of universal prosperity.

Pacem in Terris

102. . . . We think it is most opportune that as far as possible employment should seek the worker, not vice versa. For then most citizens have an opportunity to increase their holdings without being forced to leave their native environment and seek a new home with many a heartache, and adopt a new state of affairs and make new social contacts with other citizens.

A WORLD SOCIETY

THE idea that the world is a community and that individual nations are members of that community has been growing in Catholic social and political thought. Pope Pius XII repeatedly stated that worldwide inter-dependence is a fact, and that mankind should organize juridical institu-tions on a global basis. Pope John develops this same idea in more detail. He gives moral, economic, and political reasons for active solidarity among sovereign states.

First he insists that relationships between states be governed by norms based on truth and justice. Regardless of their levels of culture or eco-nomic development, nations have both rights and duties. They have the "right to existence, to self-development, and to the means necessary for this." They have the corresponding duty to respect similar rights in other countries.

The common good of individual nations cannot be divorced from the common good of the entire human family. For this reason nations should co-operate on various levels and they should permit their citizens freely to mingle with citizens of other countries. These contacts should be fostered until we finally attain peaceful relationships among all the nations of the world, "an adjustment founded on mutual trust, on sincerity in negotiations, on faithful fulfillment of obligations assumed."

The Pope is not naïvely assuming that such trust will be easy to attain. But he asks nations to aim in this direction. They should try to find some point of agreement that will be the beginning of other accords that will be "sincere, lasting, and fruitful."

There are also solid economic reasons for emphasizing the interdepend-ence of nations. Even the wealthiest communities are not self-sufficient. "They can help themselves only in so far as they succeed in helping one another." Growth in communications has brought people much closer together. The social progress of one nation, and its security and peace, are closely connected with similar goals in other countries.

Finally, there is the political fact that "today the universal common good poses problems of world-wide dimensions, which cannot be ade-quately tackled or solved except by the efforts of a public authority endowed with a wideness of powers, structure, and means of the same proportions." This means a public authority that is able to operate effectively on a world-wide basis. "The moral order itself, therefore, demands that such a public authority be established." It should be established by common agreement and not by force.

The Pope envisages this world government as similar in structure and operations to the sovereign states which brought it into being. Its first aim must be the safeguarding of the rights of the human person. It must be governed by the principle of subsidiarity. This means that it will not destroy or impair the internal sovereignty of its member nations, but rather undertake those tasks which are necessary for world order, but beyond the powers of individual nations or even groups of nations.

This part of *Pacem in Terris* caused considerable comment and confusion. Many considered the idea of a world state as utopian. Others were confused as to its relationship with the United Nations, which the Pope praised highly and encouraged to expand and prosper (No. 145).

Both difficulties can be cleared up, if we understand the evident purpose of the Pope in writing this encyclical. It was meant primarily as a majestic summary of Christian doctrine in regard to the rights and duties of the individual, the state, and the world community. It is a portrayal of the moral and political basis for world peace and harmony, as well as for internal harmony within individual nations. In this respect it can be compared to the Sermon on the Mount. That Sermon expresses the highest moral and religious ideals ever given to mankind. Few individuals or groups have lived up fully to its demands. But all have profited from striving in that direction.

This presentation of an ideal gives us a basis for evaluating the present world order and any plans for the future. Proposals that move in this direction are sound. Projects that are incompatible with it are suspect. Nor was the Pope content with merely presenting an ideal — he offers many concrete, practical, and immediate suggestions. But we should never underestimate the force of ideals. What Gandhi and Martin Luther King have done in our day should be sufficient indication of the explosive force of high aspiration.

World order, as envisioned by the Pope, might grow out of the United Nations or from some successor group, should the UN be dissolved. Human development is normally evolutionary, not revolutionary, and in this same encyclical the Pope cautions against revolution (Nos. 161–162).

Those who consider this encyclical as merely utopian must pass the same judgment against Christianity itself, since this document reflects nothing but pure Christian principles developed in the context of world problems.

POPULATION PROBLEMS

Mater et Magistra treats population problems in three phases. First, it summarizes the arguments given to prove that there is a population explosion. Next it examines from an economic viewpoint the possibilities of providing food for expanding populations, without seeking family limitation. Finally, it reiterates the Catholic position that contraception is contrary to natural law and hence is not an acceptable means for population planning.

Demographic arguments to the effect that we face a population crisis have not convinced the Pope. He questions the reliability of statistics and notes that the resources of nature are "well-nigh inexhaustible." Even when the problem seems to exist in a given area, the preferable solution is better economic and social organization, so that resources can be made available as population grows.

The encyclical rightly emphasizes that this is a problem that affects man's dignity and the immense worth of human life. To approach it merely from a statistical and demographic viewpoint, overlooking the fact that human life and families are involved, is to follow a materialistic conception of life.

On the other hand, in reacting against an overspecialized approach by demographers, we should not go to such an extreme as to attack the very science of demography. The Church does not want another Galileo case. It is a fact that world population growth is enormous and that the rate of growth is increasing. Many developing nations that aspire to quick industrialization and higher standards of living find themselves hard put to keep per capita output constant, much less to increase it. If present trends do not change, then the rich nations will get progressively richer and the poor nations will sink ever further into destitution. Quite apart from the injustice of this trend, it has ominous implications for world peace and tranquillity.

Every effort must be made, as the first and most urgent step, to foster economic, social, and political development in low-income nations, so that their living standards will rise. The splendid work of F.A.O., I.L.O., A.I.D., the Peace Corps, PAVLA, and similar technical-assistance operations should continue and be intensified. This point will be further stressed in the section to follow.

But we should not overreact to programs based on contraception and deny that there can ever be sound reasons for family limitation or population control. Pope Pius XII clearly stated that such reasons can exist, and further expressed the hope that science would ultimately be able to aid parents who seek to plan their families in a way fully in harmony with moral law.

Family planning is not coextensive with the population problem. Parents in sparsely developed areas may have personal reasons to seek to space the coming of children and to limit the over-all size of families. For example, they may be concerned over the proper education of children. The health of the mother may be a factor, as well as the economic circumstances of the family. Indications of this nature, according to many Catholic authors, make legitimate the practice of periodic abstinence for the purpose of family planning.

Pope John did not see any "immediate and imminent world problem" of starvation caused by population outgrowing world food supplies. But it could be argued that developing nations are not content today merely to hold on — they want their rightful share of the abundance made possible by modern technology. They resent putting all available resources into food production, leaving little or no capital to accumulate for industrial growth. A reading of the extremely careful formulation of the encyclical leads to the conclusion that it was not denying the sounder arguments of demographers, but rather asking mankind first to concentrate on economic, social, and political reforms.

Population control alone is purely negative. It does not change the deep-rooted social evils that are the historic reasons for poverty in so much of the world. For example, if the population of Latin America were to remain static, and social conditions were also to remain unchanged, then all we would have would be indefinite perpetuation of present levels of poverty. The Pope rightly wants a more positive and forward program.

ECONOMIC DEVELOPMENT

If the primary answer to population pressures is to be economic development, these two sections of *Mater et Magistra* are very closely interrelated. Throughout the world, there are gross disproportions between land and population. Some countries have abundant arable land and small populations. In others the situation is reversed. Some have modernized agriculture, others use primitive methods. There are food surpluses in parts of the world and shortages elsewhere. "The solidarity of the human race . . . demands the elimination as far as possible of these discrepancies." Peoples must co-operate to facilitate the movement of goods, capital, and men from one country to another. Wealthy nations have a moral obligation to help those in the process of development. Indeed, their self-interest should warn them that world peace is endangered by present imbalances.

Having established a moral judgment on the situation, the encyclical praises various types of aid that can be and often are being given. There is emergency aid for famine conditions. A more permanent type of help is technical assistance and scientific training for workers in developing nations. Then, of course, there are the development projects financed by loans and grants from "have" nations. The Pope praises what has been done and asks that these efforts be intensified.

But he warns against efforts to make these growing economies mere carbon copies of the older industrial nations that are assisting newly independent countries. The assisting nations should not impose their own mistakes on those they help, such as overstressing economic progress and neglecting social progress. Nor should the imbalance between industry and agriculture be exported to them. Aid should not be vitiated by cultural imperialism, which neglects the sound elements in ancient cultures. Even worse is tying assistance to Cold War politics, seeking political domination of the emerging nations and thus subjecting them to a new form of colonialism.

The wisdom of this analysis is self-evident and needs no clarifying comment. Two observations may be helpful, however. First, it is clear that if the principles of *Pacem in Terris* begin to take hold, and the arms race is halted, then powerful industrial nations would have much more in the way of resources to give for economic development in Asia, Africa, and Latin America. Second, we Catholics should be constantly insisting that such aid is a moral obligation. It should be given intelligently and not wasted. But it is not a bribe for political influence. Nor is it intended to buy friendship and gratitude. We may well argue that loans are better than grants, and less resented by the receiver. But we would be in a morally stronger position, and run into far fewer disappointments, if our aid were disinterested. We might even discover, as missionaries have known for centuries, that the cup of water given for love of Him is not forgotten, neither in heaven nor on this earth.

See Social Principles and Economic Life, Chapter XV, pp. 299–314.

RACIAL DISCRIMINATION AND RACIAL JUSTICE

Pacem in Terris

44. . . . the conviction that all men are equal by reason of their natural dignity has been generally accepted. Hence racial discrimination can in no way be justified, at least doctrinally or in theory. And this is of fundamental importance and significance for the formation of human society according to those principles which We have outlined above. For, if a man becomes conscious of his rights, he must become equally aware of his duties. Thus he who possesses certain rights has likewise the duty to claim those rights as marks of his dignity, while all others have the obligation to acknowledge those rights and respect them.

62. One of the fundamental duties of civil authorities, therefore, is to co-ordinate social relations in such fashion that the exercise of one man's rights does not threaten others in the exercise of their own rights nor hinder them in the fulfillment of their duties. Finally, the rights of all should be effectively safeguarded and, if they have been violated, completely restored.

86. First among the rules governing relations between political communities is that of truth. But truth requires the elimination of every trace of racism, and the consequent recognition of the principle that all states are by nature equal in dignity.

RACIAL JUSTICE

THERE never has been the slightest doubt about the strong opposition of the Holy See to racial discrimination. This has been made clear, in a private manner, to the bishops of affected areas. Solemn condemnations of racism, however, have not been frequent in papal documents, probably because racial tensions have generally been severe only in two or three nations of the world. It is providential that the strong position taken in *Pacem in Terris* came at a time when racial tensions in the United States were mounting to critical levels. Pope Paul VI repeated this stand when he received President Kennedy in audience. He stated: "We are ever mindful in Our prayers of the efforts to insure to all your citizens the equal benefits of citizenship, which have as their foundations the equality of all men because of their dignity as persons and children of God."

Since 1959, when the problem of racial discrimination was discussed in *Social Principles and Economic Life*, there has been literally a revolutionary civil-rights explosion in the United States. For the first time, the issue has been widely presented as a moral problem. American Negroes have taken the simple position that what is morally wrong should stop at once. Patience, gradualism, and selective progress are not appropriate when basic human rights are involved.

Because of this new approach, many of the distinctions offered in the 1959 book are partly dated. It remains true that the basic problems are education, job opportunity, housing, and civil rights. These are fundamental; others are peripheral. But some of these peripheral issues have become vital at the moment, mainly because they symbolize attitudes of prejudice and discrimination. Consequently we have sit-ins at lunch counters, kneels-ins at churches, and wade-ins at bathing beaches. The conviction has arisen that all discrimination, whether based on law or community customs, must go and go at once.

To achieve this result, the technique of nonviolent direct action has been the main weapon. This technique was used successfully by Gandhi, and his philosophy has inspired the Rev. Martin Luther King to use similar methods. Freedom rides, protest marches, picketing, and deliberate violation of unjust laws all have served to dramatize the Negro protest against segregation, discrimination, and racial prejudice.

THE NATIONAL CONFERENCE ON RELIGION AND RACE

Negroes have not walked alone in these demonstrations. They have been joined by many persons from the white community who have gone to jail with their Negro brothers, and, in one case at least, accepted martyrdom. Prominent among these supporters have been clergymen of all faiths, although Catholic priests have not participated so often as have ministers and rabbis in protest marches and picket lines. One of the most significant religious measures of support was the historic National Conference on Religion and Race, held in 1963. This Conference gathered top religious leaders, of every faith and race, in earnest and deep confrontation of every aspect of racial discrimination.

It was the first time in United States history that top-level leaders of all faiths convened, on their own initiative, a gathering to give a religious response to a great national moral issue. Even more significant was the decision to continue, at the local level as well as the national, this pattern of interreligious approach to racial justice. The Conference itself stimulated and directed co-ordination of national church and synagogue leadership in interracial programs, and also aided local programs in most major cities of the land. The result was a notable intensifying of interracial effort and a promotion of profound ecumenical contacts.

Local action committees under interreligious sponsorship were most successful when they were broadly representative of the community. Initial planning conferences were convened by the most prominent religious leaders of the area. Determined effort was made to be sure that all phases of opinion in the Negro community were represented in the main committee. Subcommittees were assigned for important problems, such as housing, job discrimination, school dropouts, unemployment, interracial visiting, educating the functionally illiterate, and public relations. In these subcommittees extensive use was made of various types of experts. There was informal liaison with civic groups, such as the National Urban League, the National Association for the Advancement of Colored People, the Congress of Racial Equality, the Student Nonviolent Co-ordinating Committee, and the Southern Christian Leadership Conference. But the interreligious committees kept their unity of purpose by confining direct membership to clergy and religiously active laity.

PROBLEMS TO BE FACED

It seems clear to most students of the problem that the basic issue to be faced is that of segregation. There is legal segregation in the South and de facto segregation in much of the rest of the nation. Segregated housing leads to segregated schooling. The barriers erected by these practices in turn make it more likely that there will be discrimination in job opportunities and in the use of public accommodations. The full extent of these barriers is often overlooked, even by persons who profess no racial prejudice. Such persons may have little intimate and firsthand knowledge of the problems faced by minority groups, and may have few, if any, close friendships that cross racial boundaries.

Not only does discrimination follow from segregation, but there is evidence that racial prejudice is primarily a result of the lack of meaningful contact between races. When people do not meet in a direct, personal way, there is a great danger that they regard one another in terms of stereotypes. Generalizations may be accepted that in fact are based on exceptional conduct by a minority of the group involved. Or dislikes may be grounded on surface observation, with little insight into the fundamental reasons behind the conduct in question.

This is the underlying reason for the strong drive by the Negro community for complete acceptance in all phases of American life. Understandably Negroes reject the insult implied in segregation and wish this practice removed totally. It is also clear why Negroes want to obtain their full civic rights and access to all opportunities available to other citizens. But, most important of all, they wish to be accepted as persons taking their normal positions in the social and religious life of the nation as well as in its educational, economic, and political life.

These considerations explain the scope of the demonstrations that affect virtually every aspect of the American scene. They are behind the pressures for racial balance in schools and immediate action to redress past discrimination in employment. They explain programs that may seem artificial to some persons, such as interracial visitations conducted by religious or civic groups. And they give particular urgency to the advice given to all persons who seek interracial betterment: work with the Negro people and not merely for them.

While the hoped-for results of these activities would be the virtual abolition of discrimination in the United States, many serious problems would remain, even were the crusade to meet with total success. Because of past discrimination, there are many Negroes who lack adequate education. Some are demoralized and ill-equipped to take a responsible position in civil life. The problem of restoring a sense of human dignity to those who had long been deprived of rights and opportunities is particularly a task for religious and humanitarian groups. This long-range challenge must be faced, regardless of the outcome of struggles for civil rights. See Social Principles and Economic Life, Chapter XV.

Chapter XVI

CATHOLIC RURAL PHILOSOPHY

CURRENT RURAL PROBLEMS

Mater et Magistra

123. First, with regard to agriculture, it would not appear that the rural population as a whole is decreasing, but it is an undeniable fact that many people are moving away from their farms into more thickly populated areas as well as into the cities themselves. When we realize that this movement of population is going on in nearly every part of the world, often on a large scale, we begin to appreciate the complexity of the human problems involved and their difficulty of solution.

124. We know that as an economy develops, the number of people engaged in agriculture decreases, while the percentage employed in industry and the various services rises. Nevertheless, We believe that very often this movement of population from farming to industry has other causes besides those dependent upon economic expansion. Among these there is the desire to escape from confining surroundings which offer little prospect of a more comfortable way of life. There is the lure of novelty and adventure which has taken such a hold on the present generation, the attractive prospect of easy money, of greater freedom and the enjoyment of all the amenities of town and city life. But a contributory cause of this movement away from the country is doubtless the fact that farming has become a depressed occupation. It is inadequate both in productive efficiency and in the standard of living it provides.

125. Nearly every country, therefore, is faced with this fundamental problem: What can be done to reduce the disproportion in productive efficiency between agriculture on the one hand, and industry and services on the other; and to ensure that agricultural living standards approximate as closely as possible those enjoyed by city dwellers who draw their resources either from industry or from the services in which they are engaged? What can be done to persuade agricultural workers that, far from being inferior to other people, they have every opportunity of developing their personality through their work, and can look forward to the future with confidence?

126. It seems to Us opportune to indicate certain directives that can contribute to a solution of this problem: directives which We believe have value whatever may be the historical environment in which one acts — on condition, obviously, that they be applied in the manner and to the degree allowed, suggested, or even demanded by the circumstances.

SOME REMEDIES

Mater et Magistra

127. In the first place, considerable thought must be given, especially by public authorities, to the suitable development of essential facilities in country areas — such as roads, transportation, means of communication, drinking water, housing, health services, elementary, technical, and professional education, religious and recreational facilities, and the supply of modern installations and furnishings for the farm residence. Such services as these are necessary nowadays if a becoming standard of living is to be maintained. In those country areas where they are lacking, economic and social progress is either prevented or greatly impeded, with the result that nothing can be done to retard the drift of population away from the land, and it even becomes difficult to make a good appraisal of the numbers involved.

128. If a country is to develop economically, it must do so gradually, maintaining an even balance between all sectors of the economy. Agriculture, therefore, must be allowed to make use of the same reforms in the method and type of production and in the conduct of the business side of the venture as are permitted or required in the economic system as a whole. All such reforms should correspond as nearly as possible with those introduced in industry and the various services.

129. In this way, agriculture will absorb a larger amount of industrial goods and require a better system of services. But at the same time it will provide both industry and the services and the country as a whole with the type of products which, in quantity and quality, best meet the needs of the consumer and contribute to the stability of the purchasing power of money — a major consideration in the orderly development of the entire economic system.

130. One advantage which would result from the adoption of this plan would be that it would be easier to keep track of the movement of the working force set free by the progressive modernization of agriculture. Facilities could then be provided for the training of such people for their new kind of work, and they would not be left without economic aid and the mental and spiritual assistance they need to ensure their proper integration in their new social milieu.

The need for a suitable economic policy

131. In addition, a sound agricultural program is needed if public authority is to maintain an evenly balanced progress in the various branches of the economy. This must take into account tax policies, credit, social insurance, prices, the fostering of ancillary industries, and the adjustment of the structure of farming as a business enterprise.

132. In a system of taxation based on justice and equity it is fundamental that the burdens be proportioned to the capacity of the people contributing.

133. But the common good also requires that public authorities, in assessing the amount of tax payable, take cognizance of the peculiar difficulties of farmers. They have to wait longer than most people for their returns, and these are exposed to

greater hazards. Consequently, farmers find greater difficulty in obtaining the capital necessary to increase returns.

134. For this reason, too, investors are more inclined to put their money in industry rather than agriculture. Farmers are unable to pay high rates of interest. Indeed, they cannot as a rule make the trading profit necessary to furnish capital for the conduct and development of their own business. It is therefore necessary, for reasons of the common good, for public authorities to evolve a special credit policy and to form credit banks which will guarantee such capital to farmers at a moderate rate of interest.

Social insurance and social security

135. In agriculture the existence of two forms of insurance may be necessary: one concerned with agricultural produce, the other with the farm workers and their families. We realize that agricultural workers earn less per capita than workers in industry and the services, but that is no reason why it should be considered socially just and equitable to set up systems of social insurance in which the allowances granted to farm workers and their families are substantially lower than those payable to other classes of workers. Insurance programs that are established for the general public should not differ markedly whatever be the economic sector in which the individuals work or the source of their income.

136. Systems of social insurance and social security can make a most effective contribution to the overall distribution of national income in accordance with the principles of justice and equity. They can therefore be instrumental in reducing imbalances between the different classes of citizens.

Price protection

137. Given the special nature of agricultural produce, modern economists must devise a suitable means of price protection. Ideally, such price protection should be enforced by the interested parties themselves, though supervision by the public authority cannot be altogether dispensed with.

138. On this subject it must not be forgotten that the price of agricultural produce represents chiefly the reward of the farmer's labor rather than a return on invested capital.

139. Hence, in *Quadragesimo Anno* Pope Pius XI rightly observed that "a proper proportion between different wages is also a matter of importance." He continued: "And intimately connected with this is a proper proportion between the prices charged for the products of the various economic groups, agricultural, industrial, and so forth."

140. While it is true that farm produce is mainly intended for the satisfaction of man's primary needs, and the price should therefore be within the means of all consumers, this cannot be used as an argument for keeping a section of the population — farm workers — in a permanent state of economic and social inferiority, depriving them of the wherewithal for a decent standard of living. This would be diametrically opposed to the common good.

141. Moreover, the time has come to promote in agricultural regions the establishment of those industries and services which are concerned with the preservation, processing, and transportation of farm products. Enterprises relating to other sectors of the economy might also be established there. In this case the rural population would have another means of income at their disposal, a means which they could exploit in the social milieu to which they are accustomed.

FAMILY FARMS

Mater et Magistra

142. It is not possible to determine a *priori* what the structure of farm life should be, since rural conditions vary so much from place to place and from country to country throughout the world. But if we hold to a human and Christian concept of man and the family, we are bound to consider as an ideal that form of enterprise which is modelled on the basis of a community of persons working together for the advancement of their mutual interests in accordance with the principles of justice and Christian teaching. We are bound above all to consider as an ideal the kind of farm which is owned and managed by the family. Every effort must be made in the prevailing circumstances to give effective encouragement to farming enterprises of this nature.

143. But if the family farm is not to go bankrupt it must make enough money to keep the family in reasonable comfort. To ensure this, farmers must be given up-to-date instruction on the latest methods of cultivation, and the assistance of experts must be put at their disposal. They should also form a flourishing system of co-operative undertakings, and organize themselves professionally to take an effective part in public life, both on the administrative and the political level.

144. We are convinced that the farming community must take an active part in its own economic advancement, social progress, and cultural betterment. Those who live on the land can hardly fail to appreciate the nobility of the work they are called upon to do. They are living in close harmony with Nature — the majestic temple of Creation. Their work has to do with the life of plants and animals, a life that is inexhaustible in its expression, inflexible in its laws, rich in allusions to God the Creator and Provider. They produce food for the support of human life, and the raw materials of industry in ever richer supply.

145. Theirs is a work which carries with it a dignity all its own. It brings into its service many branches of engineering, chemistry and biology, and is itself a cause of the continued practical development of these sciences in view of the repercussions of scientific and technical progress on the business of farming. It is a work which demands a capacity for orientation and adaptation, patient waiting, a sense of responsibility, and a spirit of perseverance and enterprise.

146. It is important also to bear in mind that in agriculture, as in other sectors of production, association is a vital need today — especially in the case of family farms. Rural workers should feel a sense of solidarity with one another, and should unite to form co-operatives and professional associations. These are very necessary if farm workers are to benefit from scientific and technical methods of production and protect the prices of their products. They are necessary, too, if they are to attain an equal footing with other professional classes who, in most cases, have joined together in associations. They are necessary, finally, if farm workers are to have their proper voice in political circles and in public administration. The lone voice is not likely to command much of a hearing in times such as ours.

Social responsibility

147. In using their various organizations, agricultural workers — as indeed all other classes of workers — must always be guided by moral principles and respect for the civil law. They must try to reconcile their rights and interests with those of other classes of workers, and even subordinate the one to the other if the common good demands it. If they show themselves alive to the common good and contribute to its realization, they can legitimately demand that their efforts for the improvement of agricultural conditions be seconded and complemented by public authority.

148. We therefore desire here to express Our satisfaction with those sons of Ours the world over who are actively engaged in co-operatives, in professional groups, and in worker movements intent on raising the economic and social standards of the agricultural community.

149. In the work on the farm the human personality finds every incentive for self-expression, self-development, and spiritual growth. It is a work, therefore, which should be thought of as a vocation, a God-given mission, an answer to God's call to actuate His providential, saving plan in history. It should be thought of, finally, as a noble task, undertaken with a view to raising oneself and others to a higher degree of civilization.

THE RURAL PROBLEM

THE treatment of farm problems in *Mater et Magistra* is by far the most thorough in any papal social document. In spite of this fact, there are certain unavoidable limitations to any effort to face agricultural conditions on a world scale. It is a fairly safe generalization that agriculture is in trouble throughout most of the world. But the causes of these difficulties vary from country to country, and consequently the same remedies may not be equally suitable in every area.

The Pope notes that there is a general movement from the farms to the cities. In part this is a natural consequence of industrialization. But it also stems partly from the fact that farming has become a depressed occupation. Farming is inadequate both in productive efficiency and in the standard of living it provides. This is the problem which the encyclical seeks to remedy.

Before considering these remedies, we must note that the problem does not frame itself in precisely the same terms here in the United States. Part of our agricultural economy is depressed, inefficient, and plagued by low living standards. But a substantial part is highly efficient. Many in this group have good incomes. Where efficient farmers suffer from inadequate incomes, the problem is usually one of unsalable surpluses.

Similar distinctions must be made in regard to certain of the remedies proposed. For example, it is urged that public services be made available to rural areas, so that farmers will not lack education, medical care, cultural opportunity, and means of communication. In our country there have been great advances in the area of providing public services for our farm population. Most farms today have electricity and telephone facilities. They border on good roads. Farm children go to well-staffed central schools. Medical care is often a weak point, but easy transportation to urban centers helps to make up in part for this gap.

The two million or so farms that are not fully modern may lack many of these amenities. But the problem here is both the possibility and wisdom of pouring money into such farms to modernize their equipment and train their operators, when we already have substantial surpluses in many crops. There are social reasons why we would like to retain most of these families on farms. But it may be desirable that only part of their income be derived from the sale of crops, and that the remainder be secured through seasonal work in factories located in depressed rural areas. The Office of Rural Areas Development has favored such an approach, and test projects have been successful. The encyclical favors this "fostering of ancillary industries," as well as the training of rural workers who plan to migrate to cities.

When the encyclical advocates special tax and credit policies geared to the needs of farmers, it is endorsing a program that already exists here to a substantial degree. The same point, at least in part, applies to recommendations for crop insurance and social security for farmers. Farm owners can get social security, which the Pope considers a most helpful device for distribution of national income in accordance with the principles of justice and equity. Of course, social insurance in the United States is far less extensive than that prevailing in Europe, since we lack health insurance and family allowances in our system. Moreover, most of the legal protection given to agriculture is not available to farm workers. Migrant workers in particular are at the bottom of the social and economic scale, although some modest efforts have been made to better their lot.

Price protection for farm products is strongly endorsed by *Mater et Magistra*. The encyclical holds that the desire of consumers for lower prices should not be an argument for keeping farm workers in a permanent state of economic and social inferiority. Actually, in the United States the farmer gets less than 40 per cent of the price charged the consumer. Many crops could double in price without necessarily causing any sizable price increase in the consumer product, such as bread. We in the United States generally favor the idea of price protection for many farm products. Our historic problem has been to devise a suitable system for achieving this, without piling up immense surpluses of stored products or involving the national treasury in ever increasing outlays. We accept the moral principle of giving suitable and stable incomes to farmers, but we have had considerable difficulty in working out the proper technique for implementing this principle.

THE FAMILY FARM

One of the most consistent goals of Catholic rural philosophy has been the preservation and protection of the family farm. The encyclical characterizes it simply as a "farm which is owned and managed by the family." Such farms should be aided in adopting the latest methods of cultivation. Experts should be available to assist them in their problems. They should form a flourishing system of co-operatives. Farmers of this type should organize themselves professionally to take an effective part in public life, both on the administrative and the political level.

In the United States we have been only partly successful in realizing this ideal. Many of our family farms are flourishing. But it has been charged that agricultural legislation tends to favor the ultralarge "factory farms," often owned in an absentee fashion and run by managers with the aid of hired labor. It is also charged that some of our farm organizations cater to these interests, rather than family farms. A factory farm can reduce acreage, in accordance with government programs, and still cultivate its remaining land efficiently. A one-family farm, under similar conditions, does not use its labor and equipment to the fullest extent and hence does not achieve the lowest possible costs. For this reason, groups such as the National Farmers Union and the National Catholic Rural Life Conference have often favored special legislative aids for family-type farms.

When the encyclical extols the nobility of farming, and it does this in terms of lyrical beauty, its comments apply particularly to family farms. But it realistically calls upon farm workers to associate for their own protection. Co-operative and professional associations not only help in securing the best scientific and technical methods of production, and better price protection, but they also put farmers on an equal political footing with other organized groups. "The lone voice is not likely to command much of a hearing in times such as ours." This gem of political wisdom should never be lost sight of by American farmers.

Neither should farmers overlook the admonition to subordinate their interests to the common good and to be sensitive to the needs of other types of workers. Too often American farmers have been misled by some of their spokesmen into legislative opposition to legitimate demands of urban labor. It is no accident that, of the twenty "right-to-work" states, nineteen are predominantly rural. Until the Supreme Court outlawed disproportionate rural representation in state legislatures, most state governments neglected urban needs. This was a major factor in promoting social legislation at the federal level and achieving a greater centralization of power in Washington than many persons consider desirable.

See Social Principles in Economic Life, Chap. XVI.

Chapter XVII

SOCIAL PRINCIPLES AND SOCIAL ACTION

MORAL AND SPIRITUAL CRISIS

Mater et Magistra

175. Scientific and technical progress, economic development and the betterment of living conditions, are certainly valuable elements in a civilization. But we must realize that they are essentially instrumental in character. They are not supreme values in themselves.

176. It pains Us, therefore, to observe the complete indifference to the true hierarchy of values shown by so many people in the economically developed countries. Spiritual values are ignored, forgotten or denied, while the progress of science, technology, and economics is pursued for its own sake, as though material well-being were the be-all and end-all of life. This attitude is contagious, especially when it infects the work that is being done for the less developed countries, which have often preserved in their ancient traditions an acute and vital awareness of the more important human values, on which the moral order rests.

177. To attempt to undermine this national integrity is clearly immoral. It must be respected and as far as possible clarified and developed, so that it may remain what it is: a foundation of true civilization.

210. The almost limitless horizons opened up by scientific research only go to confirm this truth. More and more men are beginning to realize that science has so far done little more than scratch the surface of nature and reality. There are vast hidden depths still to be explored and adequately explained. Such men are appalled when they consider how these gigantic forces for good can be turned by science into engines of destruction. They realize then the supreme importance of spiritual and moral values, if scientific and technical progress is to be used in the service of civilization, and not involve the whole human race in irremediable disaster.

211. Furthermore, the increasing sense of dissatisfaction with worldly goods which is making itself felt among citizens of the wealthier nations, is rapidly destroying the treasured illusion of an earthly paradise. Men, too, are becoming more and more conscious of their rights as human beings, rights which are universal and inviolable; and they are aspiring to more just and more human relations with their fellows. The effect of all this is to make the modern man more deeply aware of his own limitations, and to create in him a striving for spiritual values. All of this encourages Us in the hope that individuals and nations will one day learn

to unite in a spirit of sincere understanding and profitable co-operation.

215. Let men make all the technical and economic progress they can, there will be no peace nor justice in the world until they return to a sense of their dignity as creatures and sons of God, who is the first and final cause of all created being. Separated from God a man is but a monster, in himself and toward others; for the right ordering of human society presupposes the right ordering of man's conscience with God, who is Himself the source of all justice, truth and love.

Pacem in Terris

151. It is no less clear that today, in traditionally Christian nations, secular institutions, although demonstrating a high degree of scientific and technical perfection, and efficiency in achieving their respective ends, not infrequently are but slightly affected by Christian motivation or inspiration.

152. It is beyond question that in the creation of those institutions many contributed and continue to contribute who were believed to be and who consider themselves Christians; and without doubt, in part at least, they were and are. How does one explain this? It is Our opinion that the explanation is to be found in an inconsistency in their minds between religious belief and their action in the temporal sphere. It is necessary, therefore, that their interior unity be re-established, and that in their temporal activity faith should be present as a beacon to give light, and charity as a force to give life.

APOSTOLATE OF THE LAITY

Mater et Magistra

182. It is a source of profound satisfaction to Us to see the prominent part which is being played by Catholic citizens of the less wealthy countries in the economic and social development of their own state.

183. Then, too, the Catholics of the wealthier states are doing all they can to increase the effectiveness of the social and economic work that is being done for the poorer nations. We would give Our special approval to the increasing assistance they are giving, in all sorts of ways, to African and Asian students scattered throughout the universities of Europe and America; and to the care that is being devoted to the training of those persons who are prepared to go to the less wealthy areas in order to engage in work of a technical and professional nature.

184. To these Our beloved sons in every land who, in promoting genuine progress and civilization, are a living proof of the Church's perennial vitality, We wish to extend Our kind and fatherly word of appreciation and encouragement.

222. First, we must reaffirm most strongly that this Catholic social doctrine is an integral part of the Christian conception of life.

223. It is therefore Our urgent desire that this doctrine be studied more and more. First of all it should be taught as part of the daily curriculum in Catholic schools of every kind, particularly seminaries, although We are not unaware that in some

of these latter institutions this has been done for a long time now and in an outstanding way. We would also like to see it added to the religious instruction programs of parishes and of associations of the lay apostolate. It must be spread by every modern means at our disposal: daily newspapers, periodicals, popular and scientific publications, radio and television.

224. Our beloved sons, the laity, can do much to help this diffusion of Catholic social doctrine by studying it themselves and putting it into practice, and by zealously striving to make others understand it.

225. They should be convinced that the best way of demonstrating the truth and efficacy of this teaching is to show that it can provide the solution to present-day difficulties. They will thus win those people who are opposed to it through ignorance of it. Who knows, but a ray of its light may one day enter their minds.

226. It is not enough merely to formulate a social doctrine. It must be translated into reality. And this is particularly true of the Church's social doctrine, the light of which is Truth, Justice its objective, and Love its driving force.

227. It is vitally important, therefore, that Our sons learn to understand this doctrine. They must be educated to it.

Theory and practice

228. No Christian education can be considered complete unless it covers every kind of obligation. It must therefore aim at implanting and fostering among the faithful an awareness of their duty to carry on their economic and social activities in a Christian manner.

229. The transition from theory to practice is of its very nature difficult; and it is especially so when one tries to reduce to concrete terms a social doctrine such as that of the Church. There are several reasons why this is so; among them We can mention man's deep-rooted selfishness, the materialism in which modern society is steeped, and the difficulty of determining sometimes what precisely the demands of justice are in a given instance.

230. Consequently, a purely theoretical instruction in man's social and economic obligations is inadequate. People must also be shown ways in which they can properly fulfill these obligations.

231. In Our view, therefore, formal instruction, to be successful, must be supplemented by the students' active co-operation in their own training. They must gain an experimental knowledge of the subject, and that by their own positive action.

232. It is practice which makes perfect, even in such matters as the right use of liberty. Thus one learns Christian behavior in social and economic matters by actual Christian action in those fields.

233. The lay apostolate, therefore, has an important role to play in social education — especially those associations and organizations which have as their specific objective the christianization of contemporary society. The members of these associations, besides profiting personally from their own day-to-day experience in this field, can also help in the social education of the rising generation by giving it the benefit of the experience they have gained.

236. There are three stages which should normally be followed in the reduction of social principles into practice. First, one reviews the concrete situation; secondly, one forms a judgment on it in the light of these same principles; thirdly, one decides what in the circumstances can and should be done to implement these

principles. These are the three stages that are usually expressed in the three terms: *look, judge, act.*

237. It is important for our young people to grasp this method and to practice it. Knowledge acquired in this way does not remain merely abstract, but is seen as something that must be translated into action.

238. Differences of opinion in the application of principles can sometimes arise even among sincere Catholics. When this happens, they should be careful not to lose their respect and esteem for each other. Instead, they should strive to find points of agreement for effective and suitable action, and not wear themselves out in interminable arguments, and, under pretext of the better or the best, omit to do the good that is possible and therefore obligatory.

The Christian in the world

254. We have only been able to touch lightly upon this matter, but Our sons, the laity especially, must not suppose that they would be acting prudently to lessen their personal Christian commitment in this passing world. On the contrary, We insist that they must intensify it and increase it continually.

255. In His solemn prayer for the Church's unity, Christ Our Lord did not ask His Father to remove His disciples from the world: "I pray not that thou shouldst take them out of the world, but that thou shouldst keep them from evil." Let no man therefore imagine that a life of activity in the world is incompatible with spiritual perfection. The two can very well be harmonized. It is a gross error to suppose that a man cannot perfect himself except by putting aside all temporal activity, on the plea that such activity will inevitably lead him to compromise his personal dignity as a human being and as a Christian.

256. That a man should develop and perfect himself through his daily work — which in most cases is of a temporal character — is perfectly in keeping with the plan of divine Providence. The Church today is faced with an immense task: to humanize and to Christianize this modern civilization of ours. The continued development of this civilization, indeed its very survival, demand and insist that the Church do her part in the world. That is why, as We said before, she claims the co-operation of her laity. In conducting their human affairs to the best of their ability, they must recognize that they are doing a service to humanity, in intimate union with God through Christ, and to God's greater glory.

257. To search for spiritual perfection and eternal salvation in the conduct of human affairs and institutions is not to rob these of the power to achieve their immediate, specific ends, but to enhance this power.

Animated, too, by the charity of Christ, he finds it impossible not to love his fellow men. He makes his own their needs, their sufferings and their joys. There is a sureness of touch in all his activity in every field. It is energetic, generous, and considerate.

Pacem in Terris

147. . . . in order to imbue civilization with sound principles and enliven it with the spirit of the gospel, it is not enough to be illumined with the gift of faith and enkindled with the desire of forwarding a good cause. For this end it is necessary to take an active part in the various organiza-

tions and influence them from within.

148. But since our present age is one of outstanding scientific and technical progress and excellence, one will not be able to enter these organizations and work effectively from within unless he is scientifically competent, technically capable, and skilled in the practice of his own profession.

150. For this end it is certainly necessary that human beings carry on their own temporal activities in accordance with the laws governing them and following the methods corresponding to their nature. But at the same time it is also necessary that they should carry on those activities as acts within the moral order: therefore, as the exercise or vindication of a right, as the fulfillment of a duty or the performance of a service, as a positive answer to the providential design of God directed to our salvation. In other words, it is necessary that human beings, in the intimacy of their own consciences, should so live and act in their temporal lives as to create a synthesis between scientific, technical, and professional elements on the one hand, and spiritual values on the other.

161. There are some souls, particularly endowed with generosity, who, on finding situations where the requirements of justice are not satisfied or not satisfied in full, feel enkindled with the desire to change the state of things, as if they wished to have recourse to something like a revolution.

162. It must be borne in mind that to proceed gradually is the law of life in all its expressions; therefore in human institutions, too, it is not possible to renovate for the better except by working from within them, gradually. Pius XII proclaimed: *Salvation and justice are not to be found in revolution, but in evolution through concord. Violence has always achieved only destruction, not construction; the kindling of passions, not their pacification; the accumulation of hate and ruin, not the reconciliation of the contending parties. And it has reduced men and parties to the difficult task of rebuilding, after sad experience, on the ruins of discord.*

163. There is an immense task incumbent on all men of good will, namely, the task of restoring the relations of the human family in truth, in justice, in love, and in freedom: the relations between individual human beings; between citizens and their respective political communities; between political communities themselves; between individuals, families, intermediate associations, and political communities on the one hand, and the world community on the other. This is a most exalted task, for it is the task of bringing about true peace in the order established by God.

164. Admittedly, those who are endeavoring to restore the relations of social life according to the criteria mentioned above, are not many; to them We express Our paternal appreciation, and We earnestly invite them to persevere in their work with ever greater zeal. And We are comforted by the hope that their number will increase, especially among Christian believers. For it is an imperative of duty; it is a requirement of love. Every believer in this world of ours must be a spark of light, a center of love, a vivifying leaven amidst his fellow men: and he will be this all the more perfectly the more closely he lives in communion with God in the intimacy of his own soul.

WORK WITH NON-CATHOLICS

Mater et Magistra

239. In their economic and social activities, Catholics often come into contact with others who do not share their view of life. In such circumstances, they must, of course, bear themselves as Catholics and do nothing to compromise religion and morality. Yet at the same time they should show themselves animated by a spirit of understanding and unselfishness, ready to co-operate loyally in achieving objects which are good in themselves, or can be turned to good. Needless to say, when the Hierarchy has made a decision on any point Catholics are bound to obey their directives. The Church has the right and obligation not merely to guard ethical and religious principles, but also to declare its authoritative judgment in the matter of putting these principles into practice.

Pacem in Terris

157. The doctrinal principles outlined in this document derive from both nature itself and the natural law. In putting these principles into practice it frequently happens that Catholics in many ways co-operate either with Christians separated from this Apostolic See, or with men of no Christian faith whatever, but who are endowed with reason and adorned with a natural uprightness of conduct.

158. However, one must never confuse error and the person who errs, not even when there is question of error or inadequate knowledge of truth in the moral or religious field. The person who errs is always and above all a human being, and he retains in every case his dignity as a human person; and he must be always regarded and treated in accordance with that lofty dignity. Besides, in every human being, there is a need that is congenital to his nature and never becomes extinguished, compelling him to break through the web of error and open his mind to the knowledge of truth. And God will never fail to act on his interior being, with the result that a person, who at a given moment of his life lacked the clarity of faith or even adheres to erroneous doctrines, can at a future date be enlightened and believe the truth. For Catholics, if for the sake of promoting the temporal welfare they co-operate with men who either do not believe in Christ or whose belief is faulty because they are involved in error, can provide them either the occasion or the inducement to turn to truth.

ECONOMIC SOCIETY

WHILE the Church has favored scientific and technical progress as a means of economic development and the betterment of living conditions, it holds that these are not supreme values in themselves. They are instrumental and should be under the control of man and subordinated to his cultural and spiritual interests. Infatuation with material progress as the supreme end of life is bad enough in the more industrial countries.

Even worse, its poison is contagious and it is spreading to the newly developing nations, undermining their ancient traditions and morally based cultures. Consequently we must use every effort to keep material goods in their proper place, so that they may not destroy the foundations of true civilization.

Man is beginning to realize that material wealth alone does not make this world an earthly paradise. We are becoming more aware of our human dignity and are increasingly striving for spiritual values. This is as it should be, for, separated from God, man becomes a monster. Our Christian ideals should permeate the entirety of our lives.

In fact, *Mater et Magistra* notes, many Catholic citizens in the less wealthy nations are playing leading parts in the economic and social development of their countries. Likewise, in the wealthier states, Catholics have been doing much to assist those from poorer nations. The encyclical particularly commends aid to African and Asian students in European and American universities. While we are grateful for the fatherly words of appreciation and encouragement from Pope John, we can nonetheless cast a critical eye over our own achievements in this area. Our colleges and universities have been generous in giving scholarships to foreign students. But many such students have difficulty supporting themselves during vacation periods. Colored students are not always received into our homes. Many among us may not even realize how necessary it is to give special care and attention to such students. It is a vital work of Christian charity. It might even appeal to those anxious "to do something about communism."

SOCIAL EDUCATION

Catholic social doctrine is an integral part of the Christian conception of life. Hence it should be studied in our schools at all levels, and it should be a part of the instructional programs of parishes and associations of the lay apostolate. Seminaries in particular should provide students with the social teaching of the Church. In the United States, our performance is uneven. Catholic social-science textbooks at the elementary and high school levels are quite good and embody a well-rounded presentation of Catholic social teaching. Colleges and universities may provide such courses, but not every student chooses to take them. Many of our economics faculties pride themselves on teaching "pure science," often of the mathematical variety. One wonders whether or not econometrics actually mirrors the complex world about us, independently of its exclusion of "value systems."

Many of our seminaries are weak in social teaching, in spite of the insistent pleas of recent popes. Some do offer courses in economics and sociology. Others bring social problems into the course of moral theology or pastoral theology. Sometimes the students have study clubs to supplement the more traditional teaching. Yet many moral theology textbooks solemnly discuss the morality of dueling, but treat economic life, when they discuss it at all, in terms of eighteenth- or nineteenth-century realities. Another basic difficulty lies in the weakness of the teaching faculty. Moral theologians, to a large extent, lack economic and social sophistication.

When instruction is given, it should not be purely theoretical. Students must "gain an experimental knowledge of the subject, and that by their own positive action." Practice makes perfect, "even in such matters as the right use of liberty." "Thus one learns Christian behavior in social and economic matters by actual Christian action in those fields." One is tempted to remark that the quotations are from Pope John, not John Dewey.

Because we learn by doing, the lay apostolate has an important role to play in social education. Happily, in the United States, the national lay organizations — of men, women, and youth — have shown increasing awareness of the need for a social apostolate. Among youth groups, one must particularly commend the National Federation of Catholic College Students for initiative and apostolic zeal. Both the National Council of Catholic Men and the National Council of Catholic Women have been active in promoting racial justice and in disseminating the social teaching of the Church.

As a recommended technique, the Jocist method of "look, judge, act," is singled out in Mater et Magistra. It is clear that the Pope is giving every encouragement to the more active and dynamic movements in the Church. It is not enough to study the social teaching of the Church in an abstract way; one must also learn from the marketplace, the factories, the mines, and the farms. Currently this is being done in a most effective manner in many countries of Latin America. Clergy and dedicated laity are concentrating on immediate problems, such as removing illiteracy, setting up credit unions to counter loan sharks, helping people build houses, organizing labor unions, and assisting workers and farmers to learn the latest skills in their trades.

In the United States one might get comparable training by participating in direct-action movements for racial justice, establishing neighborhood improvement associations, encouraging high school dropouts to return for their diplomas, and teaching reading and writing to functional illiterates. Students and others could learn much by teaching religion to children of migrant workers. They would soon be drawn into broader social-action programs in that area. Self-education in urban renewal projects is also possible.

Pope John's practical wisdom shows itself in his advice to Catholics on how to handle differences of opinion regarding concrete application of principles. He urges them to differ in all charity and sincerity. They should strive more to find points of agreement than to exploit every minor area of difference. And they should never, "under pretext of the better or the best, omit to do the good that is possible and therefore obligatory." Some persons are consistently negative, caviling at weak points in social-reform movements and political organizations. They note the imperfections in labor organizations, movements for racial justice, the United Nations, and so forth, but rarely offer positive and workable suggestions for action to make this a better world. Pope John remarked to the opening of Vatican Council II that he was rather impatient with such "prophets of doom." He preferred that we put our hands to the plow, and not spend our days merely wringing them.

THE CHRISTIAN AND THE WORLD

In the same spirit, he warns against those who would lessen their commitment to the world, so as to be preserved from its evils. "Let no man therefore imagine that a life of activity in the world is incompatible with spiritual perfection. The two can very well be harmonized." The Second Commandment, love of neighbor, is like unto the First, love of God. We develop and perfect ourselves through our daily work. "The Church today is faced with an immense task: to humanize and to Christianize this modern civilization of ours." When Christians conduct their human affairs to the best of their ability, "they are doing a service to humanity, in intimate union with God through Christ, and to God's greater glory."

These are powerful words and they should be understood with the greatest of accuracy. From the beginning of Christendom, there have been those who advocated fleeing from this evil world in order to protect their souls. Unconsciously, they were spiritually selfish and unapostolic. Some went to extremes and were condemned as heretical. But others merely set their sights too narrowly and negatively, and considered religion to be a purely personal affair, with highest emphasis on avoidance of evil.

On the other hand, there is also the danger, mentioned in this encyclical, of becoming too immersed in the world. One can make peace with the world on its terms, and not in terms of the Gospel of Christ. We participate in this world, surely, but for the purpose of humanizing and Christianizing it. Otherwise we can fall into the heresy of activism, being absorbed by deeds, but failing to nourish our souls through liturgy and private prayer. Our aim must be to speak for God and through God, and not in purely human ways.

The commitment urged by the Pope does not preclude the choice of some who seek lives of contemplation in the cloister. Their prayer and sacrifice, properly directed, can be truly apostolic. Indeed, there must be some element of the contemplative in every true apostle. This is the source of the charity of Christ that "makes it impossible not to love his fellow men. He makes his own their needs, their sufferings, and their joys. There is a sureness of touch in all his activity in every field. It is energetic, generous, and considerate." These remarks, certainly auto-biographical, show how a saintly soul approaches social action.

With this type of approach, as the Pope remarks in *Pacem in Terris*, one does not lose control of one's emotions and become embittered by social injustice. There is not the temptation to use revolutionary means to achieve results. One realizes that in human institutions, "it is not possible to renovate for the better except by working from within them, gradually." Love gives us the insight to see good in everyone, so that we try to build on this good, and not destroy those who oppose us. Thus we face the immense task "of restoring the relations of the human family in truth, in justice, in love, and in freedom. . . . This is a most exalted task, for it is the task of bringing about true peace in the order established by God." This call to truly Christian social action is "an imperative of duty . . . a requirement of love." "Every believer in this world of ours must be a spark of light, a center of love, and vivifying leaven amidst his fellow men: and he will be all this the more perfectly the more closely he lives in communion with God in the intimacy of his own soul."

The above quotations are equally autobiographical and explain the extraordinary world influence of Pope John XXIII. He was active, but not an activist. He was close to God, but he looked out from the sanctuary and saw the needs of the entire world. He wrote from the heart when he penned these words, and reliable sources indicate that they went to the printer in his own handwriting. One does not comment upon such words of high inspiration; one reads, meditates, and prays that he may live up to the vocation they announce.

WORK WITH NON-CATHOLICS

The treatment of conferences with non-Catholics, in both encyclicals, is thoroughly apostolic in spirit. The earlier document is somewhat more cautious in tone, asking that Catholics do not compromise principles in such meetings, and also stressing complete docility to the authority of the hierarchy, even in practical matters. But it also notes that Catholics should be generous and unselfish in social-action contacts. They need not demand perfection, but may often be satisfied with what is good or can be turned to good.

In the later encyclical, the emphasis is still more positive. It notes that Catholic social teaching is largely based on natural law, and hence should be acceptable to all persons of good will. Then there is the beautiful passage about error and the person who errs — a real monument to the Christian optimism and the warm view of human nature of its author.

Those who have frequent opportunities to work with non-Catholics in the social-action field can testify to the accuracy of these observations. Long before ecumenicism became widespread, Catholics participating in such mixed meetings acquired deep respect and admiration for their non-Catholic colleagues. They found them to be men of high principle, honorable, zealous, and self-sacrificing. Such contacts seemed to lead naturally, when the time was ripe, to the next step of biblical, liturgical, and doctrinal discussion. Without compromise in doctrine, these Catholics saw the workings of the Spirit in men of good will. God's goodness and power are without limit, and His blessing is on those who seek Him in humility, and especially on those who find Him in their bruised and suffering neighbor.

See Social Principles and Economic Life, Chap. XVII, pp. 360–379.

INDEX OF AUTHORITATIVE STATEMENTS

GENERAL INDEX